THE STRANGLING SEA

A *13TH AGE* ADVENTURE FOR 1ST-LEVEL HEROES

BY ROBIN D. LAWS

13TH AGE IS A FANTASY ROLEPLAYING GAME BY
**ROB HEINSOO, JONATHAN TWEET,
LEE MOYER, & AARON McCONNELL**

Pelgrane Press

FiRE OPAL

www.fireopalmedia.com and www.pelgranepress.com

CREDITS

PUBLISHER
Simon Rogers

ASSISTANT PUBLISHER
Cathriona Tobin

AUTHOR
Robin D. Laws

ADDITIONAL DEVELOPMENT & DESIGN
Rob Heinsoo

ART DIRECTION
Cathriona Tobin

ARTWORK
Joshua Calloway

LAYOUT
Chris Huth

EDITING
Christopher Smith Adair

PLAYTESTERS

Kevin Elmore, Crystal Elmore, Brendon Hays, Stephan Pfuetze, Joe Bartlett, Lizzy Dimmick, Andrew Sturman, Duncan Sellars, Glenn Jones, Linda Streatfield, Chris Eng, Chris Hüth, Paul Jackson, Rachel A. Kahn, Justin Mohareb, Scott Wachter, Sascha Knippig, Miriam Giesguth, Jan Loehr, Jonas Claushallmann, Uli Claushallmann, Yohann Delalande, Leonie Caljouw, Jonna Hind, Julia Nienaber, Jan "Conlaen" Van Zon, schizoid, Thiago Ribeiro, Anthony Vieira, José Ferreira, Leandro Flores, Tim Baker, Marty Lund, Caleb Shoemaker, Kevin Robertson, Anonymous Dwarf Cleric, Christopher Fransioli, Chelsea Johnson, Rhiannon Pullin, Dave Ledvora, Lisa Hunter, Nathan Winchester, Jeff Larsen, Aditya Desai, Tanaya Nadkarni, Michael Maneval, Wesley Hatin, Mark Hutchens, Matt Goldrich, Mike Goldrich, Bill Leitzke, Ivan Ewert, Sean Krieger, Sean Clark, Jessica Hurd, Jessica Cunningham, Benjamin Witunsky, Paul Hastings, Matt Maranda, Jeff Keats, Brittany Burke, Matt Costa, Shane Bushey, Christopher J. Sniezek

SPECIAL THANKS
ASH LAW (montages), Tim Baker (great playtest notes)

TABLE OF

CONTENTS

CHAPTER ONE:

INTRODUCTION

In this *13th Age* adventure for a party of 4–6 1st-level adventurers, our heroes attempt to retrieve the enigmatic engineer Inigo Sharpe from his unfortunate imprisonment in the Stranglesea. This fantastical equivalent of our world's Sargasso Sea traps wrecked ships, strands castaways, and supports an array of dangerous animal life.

When the group finds Sharpe, they discover a man who is both more and less than they probably anticipated. Now all they have to do is get him back to the forces of a friendly icon, while avoiding those of the enemy icon who wants Inigo Sharpe for sinister purposes—or maybe just wants to kill him.

Assumptions: This adventure assumes that the PC team has already assembled and is open to missions assigned by their positive icons. If this doesn't fit your heroes' description, you may need to introduce additional bridging scenes to get them started.

Time: Groups that played the adventure in two sessions were generally not as happy as groups that stretched it out for three or four sessions.

Leveling up: The adventure assumes that you'll play at first level until you're off the weed mat. There may or may not be a grand finale as second level characters.

Adjustments: If you're playing with only three PCs, you'll want to make the battles slightly easier. Bumping all the way to seven PCs means that you should add a bit more than another PC's worth of monsters; you'd probably be fine making the battles as tough as they would need to be for eight PCs because of the high number of synergies in a seven-character adventuring party.

GENERAL NOTES

Unless otherwise indicated, any time the text calls for an ability-based check, players can apply the bonuses from relevant backgrounds to those checks.

GMs who make sure they offer the PCs an incremental advance after each successful session may find that the PCs have become capable of handling each battle handily without any real threat. What the incremental advance provides, slightly tougher battles can render necessary, so feel free to adjust the opposition upward if the PCs are kicking butt too easily.

If the PCs are already second level, you're going to need to adjust the stats of all the monsters. Add +1 to every defense and attack. Bump up the damage. Look at how the monster's hit points compare to its second level and raise them a similar amount higher or lower than the base hit points of creatures at their new level.

SELECTING THE PATRON AND ANTAGONIST

This adventure pits the heroes against forces connected to an enemy icon, the **antagonist**, on behalf of operatives or agents of a heroic or ambiguous icon, the **patron**, who offers gifts to the party to start the adventure, and further rewards if they succeed in rescuing Inigo Sharpe.

The choice of patron: Before you shift from the chat phase of your opening session to the game proper, ask all the players to roll their dice for any positive relationships to heroic or ambiguous icons. (If your players have already played *13th Age*, you may want to explain that this isn't a normal icon relationship roll; it's an element of setting up the adventure.) Tally the 5s and 6s rolled in association with each icon. If one icon has more of them than any other, that's the friendly icon who will provide the PCs' patron. If the result is a tie, including one in which all icons are tied at 0, ask the players for another round of rolls. Keep rolling, until one icon accrues a higher total than all the others. An NPC connected to that icon will be your patron, as detailed in "The Patron's Story" below.

The choice of antagonist: Now repeat the exercise for each negative relationship to a villainous or ambiguous icon. Omit an ambiguous icon already chosen as patron. The icon getting the most 5s and 6s is the one whose NPC follower provides your antagonist. See "The Antagonist's Story" below for details on this servant of the enemy icon.

Alternatively: Improv-averse GMs can just choose a friendly icon and enemy icon in advance, as creative inspiration, or already established events in your campaign, dictate. You could also figure out the PCs' icon relationships and have them roll to set up the patron and antagonist before game night so that you can plan ahead instead of figuring things out on the spot.

THE INIGO SHARPE STORY

No matter whom you end up with as your patron and antagonist, some basic facts about Inigo Sharpe remain the same. The characters get the chance to learn some of these facts very soon, probably from the patron, but we're telling you now to make better sense of the next section.

- Inigo Sharpe is a famous architect, inventor, magician, and seer.
- In his prime, various heroic icons vied for his services.
- Though highly sought, he inevitably wore out his welcome with his impertinence and eccentricity.

- A few years ago, several months after a falling out with the patron icon, he vanished from sight.
- Various contradictory rumors explain this disappearance. Most say one of the hostile icons had him murdered, though the blame shifts depending on the allegiances of the rumormonger.
- As the PCs will only discover after overcoming the Stranglesea's many obstacles, Sharpe's consciousness now resides in a clockwork head. (This adds to the challenge of finding him, as the adventurers will be searching for a human-sized captive.)

The rest of Sharpe's backstory varies depending on who wants to rescue him (your patron, as chosen above) and who wants to kill or pressgang him (the antagonist).

THE ANTAGONIST'S STORY

Each of the possible enemy icons below provides an antagonist: an NPC representative of the icon who may make the PCs' lives difficult while functioning mostly behind the scenes. If your campaign has already established a suitable villain connected to the chosen icon, swap in your villain as the antagonist.

Note that the antagonist is not intended to show up onscreen during this adventure. The antagonist's agents will seek to end the PCs' lives, but the antagonist is higher level and probably too busy with more immediate problems to make hunting down Sharpe their priority. If the PCs succeed in thwarting the antagonist's revenge, they'll probably become an enemy who will reappear later in the campaign.

Sharpe designed a mighty weapon for use against demons, a whirring, telescoping combination of two-handed sword and battle axe. Dubbed *Hornharrow*, it sends demons howling back to the Abyss on a single blow. It only works when wielded by one who is pure of heart. Unfortunately for Sharpe, it was commissioned by Crusader retainer **Vitunati**, Third Reach Captain of the Blackfall Reconquest, who in a well-publicized test proved himself anything but. His hand mangled by the rebellious weapon, Vitunati suppressed all existing prototypes and ordered Sharpe killed. He thinks Sharpe is dead but, when he finds out that he isn't, will send warriors to finish the job.

Sharpe designed a weapon for use against demons, a wand that spits energy beams that send them howling back to the Abyss. The Diabolist's cleverer demonic servitors, led by a vrock named **Adrex**, learned of this and attacked his laboratory. They destroyed it, killing Sharpe, along with his colleagues and family. When Adrex gets wind of Sharpe's inexplicable survival, she sends more minions to finish the job.

Sharpe designed a weapon for use against the undead, a wand that spits energy beams robbing them of their unliving animation. When a vampire named **Vardia** caught wind of this, she hired mortal mercenaries to sack and burn Sharpe's laboratory. Distracted by a fight over plunder, the mercenaries left Sharpe for dead, failing to finish him off.

Sharpe designed a magical trap that can be laid along a frontier to cheaply deal mass casualties to an invading force. Orc chieftain **Ursorg** attacked the fort he was working from, killing dozens of brave warriors who stood between him and Sharpe. Having crushed the puny inventor man's skull with his own bare hands, Ursorg reacts to news that he might have resurfaced by ordering underlings to capture him and bring him back for an encore performance.

Sharpe once bragged that he could devise a scrying machine that could read the words of sharpers, gangsters, and criminals as they are written. Though many of the Prince's followers are illiterate, others are not. The human assassin **Sullus** caught wind of this and disposed of Sharpe—or so he thought. He has informants spying on the patron who sends the PCs on the mission. Learning from them that Sharpe might yet live, he sends underlings to learn if this is the case.

Sharpe designed a weapon for use against dragons, a wand that reveals them in their assumed human forms. Getting wind of this, the dragon **Kasta**, a medium blue, led her minions to burn his laboratory. As sifting through charred ruins does not befit a dragon's dignity or propensity for manual manipulation, Kasta's human servitors performed this task. And none too well, it turns out. She has informants spying on the patron who sends the PCs on the mission. Informed by them that Sharpe might be alive, Kasta sends underlings to track him down.

THE PATRON'S STORY

Having selected your primary baddie, decide why the patron cares about finding and rescuing Inigo Sharpe.

The simplest answer may work: The simplest story is that the patron and the antagonist are already at odds. Use one of the named patrons below and for motivation say that the patron wants the weapon mentioned in the antagonist's story.

This becomes less convincing if your antagonist is not the natural enemy of the patron, in which case you might invent a previously hidden conflict between them. For example: *Followers of the High Druid don't typically treat those of the Three as enemies. But minor dragons pledging fealty to the Blue appear to have been conducting experiments that threaten nature's balance, giving High Druid types an unexpected need for a device that exposes their true forms.*

Or go with a more complex story with more hooks: Roleplaying storylines sometimes benefit from the raggedness of intersecting plots. Yes, Inigo Sharpe is the type of guy to create multiple problems for himself! You might see more potential story threads in a patron story only tangentially related to the antagonist's agenda.

The detailed examples of the patron interactions in the "Getting the Mission" section below start out by not caring that much about the identity of the antagonist. You can alter them if you wish. You can also use one of the NPC patrons listed if you opted for the simplest answer above, outright opposition to the enemy icon and the antagonist.

The First Scene:
GETTING THE MISSION

However you have chosen the patron's motivation, the adventure begins when the patron asks the PCs to visit them in the patron's headquarters. In each case, the visit begins with a gift of a true magic item to a PC deemed worthy by the patron, followed up by a request that the PCs track down Inigo Sharpe. We'll start by covering the elements of the interaction that vary depending on the icon that the patron serves. After the icon-by-icon rundown of the protagonists, their possible gifts, and how they discovered that Inigo Sharpe was still alive, we'll cover the basic mission setup that is pretty much the same no matter who the patron is.

Do you own the Book of Loot*?:* Feel free to replace the magic items gifted below with something fun and appropriate from the icon's chapter.

Do the PCs have a headquarters?: Set the introduction near where the group makes its base. The patron or the patron's agents know where to find them and initiate contact.

Or are the PCs rootless wanderers?: Start near the usual location of the patron's icon.

FUTURE DEVELOPMENTS

If your players become interested in the details of the patron's problem and Sharpe's activities, there's a chance that a follow-up adventure could spin out of any of these patron stories. That might also be true if a second patron contacts the PCs after the end of this Stranglesea adventure, looking to solve a problem that Inigo Sharpe left them.

WORKING FOR THE ARCHMAGE

Larto, a senior instructor in the School of Imperial Wizardry, sees himself as mentor to Sharpe. Despite a break caused by Sharpe's disobedience to the sorcerous hierarchy, Larto has heard that Sharpe is in trouble and wants to protect him—whether Sharpe likes it or not.

Alternate patron: Sharpe worked as a tutor at the School of Imperial Wizardry. When he left, he stole a magical crystal key to a colleague's latest levitation experiment. The fellow tutor, **Attra**, suspects that Sharpe stashed it somewhere, probably along with other irreplaceable implements stolen from the school. Attra wants to know the location of this cache.

Sharpe lives: The patron summoned an imp to question on an originally unrelated matter, which he or she is not at liberty to discuss. (Perhaps this holds the seed of a future adventure.) Resisting telling the wizard its secrets, the imp proclaimed that it had recently received a much better offer from Inigo Sharpe. Therefore, Sharpe is alive, somewhere. And probably hiding. And needs to be found before his enemies finish the job.

The patron's gift: Larto or Attra will gift the PC whom they see as the most powerful spellcaster in the group with an adventurer-tier magic wand, probably a *wand of the mage's invisible aegis* or *wand of the unfettered minion* from page 292 of the *13th Age* core rulebook unless you have treasure you'd rather use from another sourcebook. If the PC spellcaster happens to be someone who can't use a wand, they should pass it on to someone who can use it, or plan to multiclass as a wizard soon. Hint hint.

FETCHING FOR THE CRUSADER

If Inigo Sharpe is the inventor people say he is, surely he can create a new weapon for use against demons. That means he should be slaving away for the Crusader, under the supervision of the ambitious **Vitunati**, Third Reach Captain of the Blackfall Reconquest. Unusually political for a Crusader retainer, Vitunati regards most of his peers as naïve brutes who understand only combat. There is more than one way, he explains, to flay a demon.

Alternate patron: Hard-bitten, laconic **Jothreen**, Lieutenant of the Lightning March Raiders, has found a sealed crypt full of captured demons. Sealed for now, that is. Its complex brass vault mechanism weeps and bleeds, on the verge of breaking open. She needs someone to refurbish the door without accidentally freeing its demonic prisoners. Her advisers tell her that Sharpe is the man for the job.

Sharpe lives: While researching past efforts at new anti-demon magics, Vitunati or Jothreen found a letter from an alchemist to a maker of constructs, introducing Sharpe as a trustworthy associate, dated a year after Sharpe's supposed death.

The patron's gift: The patron gifts one PC who has an icon relationship with the Crusader with an adventurer-tier magic melee weapon. Choose something fun. Make clear that Sharpe himself is not to be harmed with this weapon or any other, but he must be brought back, either willingly or as a captive.

AS THE DWARF KING COMMANDS

One of the Dwarf King's explorers, **Geta**, has found an ancient dwarven invention. To her frustrated shame, she can't work out what it is supposed to do. Since it's large and built of expensive parts, it must be important. If she can get Sharpe to identify it for her, it will do more to secure her rise through the dwarven chain of command.

Alternate patron: A swarm of mechanical gold-eating bugs has infested the dwarven mine run by the unusually handsome, charismatic dwarf mining boss **Dermon**. The King brooks no interruption to his gold supply. A desperate Dermon seeks someone to invent another mechanical bug to eat these mechanical bugs.

Sharpe lives: Geta or Dermon risked the wrath of the notoriously querulous dwarven oracle Glomus to ask who might solve the problem. The answer: "Inigo Sharpe, who is lost but not gone."

The patron's gift: Geta has a pair of magic boots that she has found useful but can't bear to wear anymore. *Boots of elvenkind* from page 289 of the core rulebook! She gives them to the closest thing the party has to an elf.

Dermon, as patron, gives a pair of magic gloves to the *dwarfiest* of the PCs. Whichever gloves you choose, they don't enjoy the miner's life, and they've been bugging him to find them a new owner who will use them gloriously instead of in the mine.

THE ELF QUEEN'S CALL

The elf noble **Jaria**, in her perpetual hunt for caprice, once invited Sharpe to stage for her a Masque of Mechanical Wonders, which, despite a certain crude élan, she found distasteful. Now one of the construct creatures he made has powered back on and ravages her grounds. Efforts of her retainers, admittedly inexpert in engineering matters, have failed. Were news of this to reach Court, Jaria would suffer embarrassment. She seeks Sharpe to disarm the device.

Alternate patron: Lithe and raven-haired, elven marchioness **Bratha** looks like an adolescent but carries herself with the weary air of one who has seen everything. The Dwarf King, as represented by the mining magnate Dermon, has starting digging for gold in elven-occupied lands. She wishes to revive a project Sharpe once proposed to her, but for which she saw no use at the time: the construction of gold-eating mechanical bugs to infest the mine.

Sharpe lives: To confirm that Sharpe was dead, the patron dropped a lotus petal in a mixture of rosewater and tarragon, with two drops of fairy blood and a hair she took the liberty of taking from Sharpe years ago. The lotus petal did not sink, revealing that Sharpe somehow escaped his supposed doom. Sadly the hair was consumed by the ritual and in any case was too degenerate to support a full tracking ritual.

The patron's gift: Jaria or Bratha would both initiate contact with the same gift, an *elven cloak* from page 289 of the core rulebook. Jaria gifts it to the PC with the highest Charisma. Bratha gives it to the PC with the highest Wisdom.

IN HIS IMPERIAL MAJESTY'S SERVICE

Inigo Sharpe once boasted to Imperial Treasury Sub-Minister **Donson Trisu** that he could build a machine to increase flour yield from mills by up to twenty-three percent. Recently transferred to the disbursement department, Donson seeks a way of impressing his superiors by squeezing additional yield from military grain supplies. When word reaches him of Inigo Sharpe's survival, he enlists his contact among the heroes to retrieve him and put him to work.

Alternate patron: The gray-haired retired general **Osren** moves with difficulty, wincing with pain from the unhealable wounds she sustained in the last war. She wishes to revive a scheme of Sharpe's she rejected as a younger, haler woman, because it did not suit the sense of martial dignity she once held so dear. Sharpe proposed a censer whose fumes would creep across the countryside, destroying any undead minions of the Lich King they came into contact with. Now valuing efficiency over honor, Osren wants Sharpe back to kick the plan back into action.

Sharpe lives: Donson or Osren found an Imperial intelligence report containing a letter from an alchemist to a maker of constructs, introducing Sharpe as a trustworthy associate, dated a year after Sharpe's supposed death.

The patron's gift: It's important to the Empire that this mission succeed, so Donson or Osren provides a gift of an adventurer-tier *lifestone necklace* (page 290 of the core rulebook).

Donson gives it to a PC with a positive or conflicted relationship with the Emperor. Osren gives it to the PC with the most hit points.

FOLLOWING THE WYRM

The medium gold dragon **All-Rise** has learned of Sharpe's work on a weapon of special efficacy against demons. She seeks the PCs' aid in adding Sharpe to her retinue.

Alternate patron: The prolix lizardman **Galadon** fears that Wyrmblessed, the floating cloud city of dragons that overhangs part of the Imperial capital of Axis, is losing its ephemeral substance. Sharpe once boasted to him that he could devise a machine that would multiply Wyrmblessed's grandeur tenfold. He wants him tracked down, to get him to work assuring its continued structural integrity.

Sharpe lives: All-Rise's special draconic power: her hunches are never wrong. And she has a hunch that Sharpe still lives.

Alternately, Galadon, friendly with the Imperial government, asked for intelligence on Sharpe's whereabouts and received the letter mentioned in the Emperor entry.

The patron's gift: All-Rise gives a shiny golden adventurer-tier magic shield to a character who can use it well.

Alternately, Galadon gives an adventurer-tier magical helmet or crown to the character who seems to him to be the leader.

THE HIGH DRUID'S CALL

Maniacal derro have surfaced to attack a pristine wilderness guarded by the druid **Feras**. They wield strange alchemical devices that flatten hillsides, turn thriving vegetation into mush, and blot out the sun with choking clouds. Feras and other druids now know that the derro aim to transform the wilderness into a version of their subterranean homeland, ripe for colonization. Feras knows nothing of derro-machinery, but remembers a brief encounter with Inigo Sharpe during a trying visit to Axis. Feras asks his contact to find Sharpe and enlist his aid.

Alternate patron: Imperial farmers have begun to clear-cut a forest overseen by the weather-beaten, raspy-voiced ranger **Redford**. Having once driven Sharpe out of his woodland for harvesting rare metals from its soils, he knows the artificer's prowess. He wants Sharpe to construct for him a series of traps that will encourage the heedless farmers to leave his lands alone. For that, he might even be willing to let him dig for his precious meteorites—under careful supervision.

Sharpe lives: Feras captured a blind derro seer, who told him that his only hope for victory lay beyond his grasp—a man who is not dead, but so lost that he might as well be so. Everyone knows that a blind derro seer cannot lie while taunting a captor. His best assumption is that the seer referred to Sharpe.

Alternately, Redford learned of Sharpe's survival by consulting a limpid lake at the heart of his forest. In its magical reflection, he beheld a vision of Sharpe.

The patron's gift: Feras provides the PC who seems to him to be most in touch with nature with adventurer-tier light armor made of magically blessed rock slates that amount to a *stone flesh* enchantment (page 287).

Alternately, Redford provides one of the party's ranged-weapon users with three precious black arrows enchanted with *lethal strike* (also page 287).

IN THE NAME OF THE PRIESTESS

Inigo Sharpe briefly worked for the abbess **Panutha**, loyal servant of the Priestess, installing alarms against the attacks of automatons and constructs in her nunnery. After a falling out over payment, he abandoned his post. As he left, he installed in the door to the abbey's relic crypt a complex lock only he can open. Now that she's heard he might still be alive, she wants that unlocked.

Alternate patron: White-haired and wise, **Ulisse**, a priestess of the gateway between life and death, drifts into occasional distraction as she speaks. She can't help seeing the ghosts of the recent dead make their slow procession to the mysteries beyond. Recently she saw the shade of her daughter-in-law, the antiquarian Reloka, who described her murder by battle-maddened Crusader soldiers. Ulisse wishes to find them and smite them with a weapon that will drain all anger and violence from their hearts, turning them to the Priestess and away from the Crusader. The only problem—the weapon was designed by Inigo Sharpe, but has not yet been built.

Sharpe lives: The patron went to bed praying to her deities for assistance, and woke up having distinctly heard the words "Inigo Sharpe lives" whispered in both ears.

The patron's gift: Neither Panutha nor Ulisse would have much personal use for an adventurer-tier magical melee weapon, but surely a PC with at least one relationship point would have a use for it on this mission.

WORKING FOR THIS GUY A FRIEND KNOWS

Rumor has it that Sharpe devised a simple device, which could be hidden on the body as jewelry, to shield the wearer's thoughts and actions from all magical observation. This would be a natural prize for up-and-coming burglar **Maxippa the Swift** to offer to the Prince of Shadows—or a higher-ranking criminal hoodwinking her by posing as the Prince of Shadows.

Alternate patron: The puckish **Irinso** wants to hear everyone's stories, and to tease them once he's identified their sore spots. Through this habit he learned of the antagonist's plans for Sharpe, whom he had not before heard of but has now researched in detail. A true trickster, Irinso's best schemes always comes to him as he goes along. He doesn't know why Sharpe will come in handy, but a hunch tells him that disrupting the enemy's plan will lead to a big score. If he can't think of anything, he can always ransom Sharpe off to the very antagonist he's planning to thwart!

Sharpe lives: If asked, the patron says the heroes don't need to know how she or he knows. Inigo Sharpe is alive and missing, and that's all that matters.

The patron's gift: Well …. In this case, the PCs aren't given a true magic item. But a few minutes after leaving Maxippa or Irinso, the most earnest PC discovers that one of their normal pieces of equipment has been stolen and switched with a quite-interesting adventurer-tier magic item that has the word *HA!* magically etched into it somewhere.

THE PATRON MEETING: ANY ICON

However and wherever they meet the patron, the heroes are likely to learn all or most of the following:

- Why the patron seeks Inigo Sharpe ("The Patron's Story," above).
- How the patron found out that Sharpe still lives, unless roleplaying interactions lead away from the topic.
- That the patron found a spy in his or her operation shortly after learning about Sharpe. Interrogation revealed whom the spy worked for, and that the spy passed knowledge of Sharpe's survival to his handlers, the antagonist. So time may matter.
- If it makes sense and will improve the story, the patron may even have an idea of why the antagonist is so keen to get hold of Sharpe, in which case a piece of "The Antagonist's Story" could be dropped into the story as an extra hook.
- If pressed, the patron isn't certain of why their own magic, or the magic of allied spellcasters, can't get a precise bead on Sharpe's current location. There's something interfering, certainly.
- Before his disappearance, Sharpe maintained a friendship with an itinerant magician named Firigin. To find Sharpe, the group might start with Firigin. The patron's magic has just been successful determining Firigin's current location: he's near a remote bay named Silver Cove on the shore of the Midland Sea between New Port and Shark Tooth Bay. Firigin's house is painted white, and very round. That should be enough to find him.

If the group has fewer than three healing potions between them, the patron also gives them enough adventurer-tier healing potions to get them up to that number.

CHAPTER TWO:

SHORELINE INVESTIGATIONS

This chapter assumes that the PCs take the patron's suggestion and look for Firigin near the Silver Cove. If the PCs pursue other routes, see the "We Can Do This Ourselves" sidebar below.

TRAVEL MONTAGE

Silver Cove is somewhere on the southwestern shore of the Midland Sea near New Port unless your campaign suggests a better location. Play out the journey from the PCs' starting location with travel montage.

Start with a player who is comfortable improvising and ask them to describe a problem that the party faces along the way. Don't let them solve the problem: turn to the player on the starting player's left and ask *them* how their player character does something clever or awesome to solve the problem. After that solution, ask that same player to describe the *next* obstacle that nearly derails the adventurers' journey. The player to their left gets to solve the new problem, and so on around the table until everyone has invented and solved a problem.

Encourage players to draw on any aspect of their character or invent something new, but don't call for any die rolls, even when the solution to a travel-hassle involves combat. These events occur in quick narrative time, and allow the players to invent small stories to reinforce their characters' defining qualities, whether these be icon relationships, unique things, or backgrounds. The vignettes that come out of the montage will often introduce elements that get called back into the story later on.

For example, the players from Robin's playtest might create problems and solutions like so:

Problem: "There are goblins scuttling on the horizon. Oh no, they're coming closer."

Solution: "No problem! I use my robot senses to pinpoint their location. Then I emit the recorded cry of a dragon. The goblins pelt away in fear."

Problem: "This forest we're going through just got threatening. There's a wolf pack, a huge flock of ravens, and a herd of moose, and they're all following us through the trees and getting closer."

Solution: "I play my bagpipes and sing the songs of the woodland choir. I inspire the animals of the wood to treat us as friends."

Problem: "We've reached a crossroads in a swamp. The signs are all destroyed. We've got no idea which way to go."

Solution: "I smell brimstone to the north. We're going south."

Problem: "Local hoodlums challenge us as we walk through a village."

Solution: "I punch the biggest one in the face. One-shot. His pals scatter."

WE CAN DO THIS OURSELVES

PCs who ignore the hint to search for Firigin might attempt to track down Inigo Sharpe using their own resources. If finding Sharpe without Firigin's help was easy, or even somewhat possible, the patron and the antagonist would have managed it already, so you have every right to rule that the muddling effect of the Stranglesea will prevent rituals or spirit inquiries arranged by the PCs.

On the other hand, if you're so impressed with the PCs' efforts that you want them to succeed without dealing with Firigin, reward them by deciding that they've accomplished what the other agents of the icons have failed: pegging Sharpe's location as the Stranglesea.

Arranging transport to the Stranglesea could be a different matter. There may be some groups with nautical resources that suggest that they can get themselves to the Stranglesea without the magical boat created by Firigin. If your group is one of those rare groups, you may wish to reward them for their uniqueness or backgrounds rather than going through the story of the magic boat. You're on your own until the PCs get to the Stranglesea because our story runs through Firigin.

FIRIGIN'S DOME

With the information provided by the patron's magic, Firigin is not that hard to find. He is living in a dome-shaped structure cut into the side of a remote, rocky hill.

When the PCs arrive, they find that the dome is under siege by minions of the antagonist icon's representative! Good timing. The thugs are trying to batter the doors and windows in, and starting to succeed, but the dome is built of something strong and isn't breaking easily.

HUMAN SELLSWORD

1ˢᵗ level troop [HUMANOID]
Initiative: +3

Short sword +5 vs. AC—5 damage

R: Darts +4 vs. AC—4 damage

Fast strike: Opponents engaged with the human sellsword take 1 damage each time they attempt to disengage (successful or otherwise).

AC	16	
PD	13	**HP 27**
MD	12	

HUMAN CLUB THUG

1ˢᵗ level spoiler [HUMANOID]
Initiative: +3

Club +5 vs. AC—4 damage
  Natural even hit: Armor wrecker! The club thug reduces the opponent's AC by 1 till end of battle.

R: Darts +4 vs. AC—3 damage

AC	16	
PD	13	**HP 27**
MD	12	

HUMAN HEDGE WIZARD

1ˢᵗ level caster [HUMANOID]
Initiative: +3

Dagger +4 vs. AC—3 damage

R: Fire jet +4 vs. PD (one nearby or far away enemy)—4 damage
  Natural even hit: Each enemy nearby the target takes 1 spillover damage.

AC	16	
PD	12	**HP 26**
MD	15	

HUMAN DART THROWER

1ˢᵗ level archer [HUMANOID]
Initiative: +4

Dagger +4 vs. AC—4 damage

R: Darts +5 vs. AC—5 damage

Opportunistic throw: When the human dart thrower is not engaged, any opponents take 1 damage each time they make a move action (explain this to players when this first happens, so they can take countermeasures).

AC	16	
PD	12	**HP 27**
MD	13	

The bad guys: Even if your antagonist usually uses monstrous henchmen, feel free to use a hired gang of toughs in this case, minions who can travel a civilized area without rousing significant alarm. The informal leader of the henchmen is a hedge wizard who calls herself Nadda. She's your classic knuckleheaded criminal who blames the world when anything goes wrong for her.

The thugs' various 1-point damage effects are meant to memorably annoy the players, making victory all the sweeter when it comes.

Firigin's Dome Fight Chart

Number of PCs	Human Sellswords	Human Club Thugs	Human Hedge Wizard	Human tDart Throwers
4	1	1	1	1
5	2	1	1	1
6	2	2	1	2

BATTLE OUTCOMES

Unlikely defeat: Defeat to such weaklings is nigh inconceivable, but if that word doesn't mean what we thought it means, have Firigin save the day with one of his own strange inventions that you make up on the spot. The device has serious consequences, probably something like burning out a magic item in the area or a similar small defeat for the PCs.

Victory: As a PC strikes down the last thug, ask that PC to make a DC 15 Wisdom skill check to notice one of the thugs that appeared to be down pulling out a healing potion. Backgrounds involving observation or military tactics should help. Success indicates the PC notices in time to get the healing potion out of the thug's hands; add one potion. Failure indicates that the potion gets spilled all over the thug in the struggle; they don't drink it cleanly, but it's gone.

HENCHMAN INTERROGATION

If defeated but kept alive for interrogation, Nadda (or another survivor with a name such as Risol, Monis, Longstack, or Qure) spills the following, in response to specific questions from the PCs:

- They have nothing against Firigin or against the heroes; they're just doing this for money.
- They're getting paid a few silver coins—a handsome fee! Uh no, they weren't paid yet. They asked for half up front but didn't get it, and something told them not to press the issue.
- They got the job from a thin human woman in a black cloak and hood at a crossroads outside New Port. The woman said she'd find them when she wanted a report, and not to bother looking for her themselves.
- The woman warned them servants of the [patron's icon] might interfere with them, but that she herself was on the way to slay several of those servants who were due to be delayed by [insert one of the stories from the travel montage if it can make sense as part of a plot set up by the antagonist].
- They were supposed to grab Firigin and see if he knew anything about someone named Inigo Sharpe. And then keep him alive until the woman in black found them.

The woman in black is a servant of the antagonist and won't appear in this adventure. She's meant as a loose end that you can bring back into play in future adventures, or not. As far as our concept of the adventure is concerned, there's not much the PCs can do to track her down.

GETTING INSIDE THE DOME

After the PCs defeat the thugs, a grateful Firigin will thank them for their timely intervention. He still may not want to ask them in, but after some suspicion and resistance, he can be convinced to unlock his nearly shattered door and invite the heroes into the modestly wondrous home of a reclusive minor magician. If you want to roll for this interaction instead of just roleplaying it, have the group's leader attempt a DC 15 Charisma skill check. Failure with the check should follow our standard fail-forward pattern (*13th Age* core book, page 42)—failure indicates the PCs still talk their way in, but Firigin will lie about a couple things and won't provide any assistance other than the secrets of the silver boat.

Firigin is a silver-haired man with shockingly white artificial teeth. He made them. He's proud of them. This is probably not a common thing in the Dragon Empire, not with this degree of perfect shape. (If you must know, the magic item's quirk is that you are horrified to eat any food that might lead to tooth decay.)

But enough about magical teeth. Firigin isn't that keen on volunteering information, but, in response to specific questions, he's willing to say all of the following:

- He and Inigo were partners, once.
- Firigin's own work as an inventor is mostly behind him. He'd rather paint watercolors, and this coastline is good for it.
- Of course he's lying a little about that, or perhaps being modest, because the windowless white dome he is living in is extremely unusual. If asked nicely, he'll say that the dome is from the same philosophy of precise mastery of simple forms to provide optimal health benefits that he employed to create his perfect artificial teeth. If the characters' eyes haven't glazed over here, credit them for diplomacy.
- Firigin marveled at Sharpe's boldness in defying one powerful employer after another. When asked how he could be so brave, Sharpe claimed to always have at least two brilliant escape plans from any situation.
- His greatest escape, he once hinted, while in his cups, would allow him to sidestep mortality itself. Provided he mastered a few minor technical points ....
- Inigo left in a huff from their mutual employer's service without preparing Firigin. Worse, the mess he left behind made it look like Firigin had helped him abscond with valuable supplies. Firigin had to face the employer's wrath, and barely escaped with his hide intact. In fact, he still bears a grievous wound as a memento of Sharpe's thoughtless betrayal. It's in a spot covered by clothes.
- After talking his way out of worse punishment, Firigin retreated here, to a life of solitary study and contemplation. He never liked people much, and his experience with Sharpe confirmed once and for all that he'd be happier alone.
- Although, in his early days here, Firigin did plot revenge against Sharpe. But even as he worked on the device that would narrow his hunt for Sharpe, the goddess of mercy entered his heart. On that fortunate day, he realized that petty revenge would bear him no fruit. So he abandoned his plan for revenge, even though he'd succeeded with the device that might accomplish it. Since then he has known peace.

- The device? During their time together, he and Sharpe worked on a project for a frivolous lord—a magical boat that would seek out its owner. Firigin built another boat, but this one he set up to home in on Sharpe if Sharpe were anywhere near the sea or attached rivers.
- The boat still exists. To activate the boat to seek out Sharpe, all you have to do is sing a certain song.
- But before Firigin tells them which song activates the boat, the heroes must promise not to harm Inigo Sharpe. Firigin doesn't want to disturb his hard-won peace by exacting even an indirect vengeance against his old betrayer. And on second thought, also promise to try to keep Inigo away from Firigin, who would rather not have to deal with the miscreant ever again.
- Promises made, Firigin reveals that the boat is hidden beneath a tarp several hundred yards from the water of Silver Cove. The boat has never been noticed because it's also concealed by several illusion spells that Firigin acquired from gnomes who owed him a favor. To get the illusion spells to drop, someone needs to loudly proclaim one secret that they would rather not make public. Seriously. (Though of course the person could be alone when they speak, a fact Firigin won't volunteer.) After the boat is carried to the water, its Inigo-tracking magic can be activated by singing an in-key rendition of the *Ballad of the Stone Girl*, an old dwarven song about a woman whose hard-heartedness matched Firigin's opinion of Inigo. Any bard, dwarf, or character with a relationship point with the Dwarf King will know the song. Others could make a DC 15 Intelligence skill check to be able to remember the song, or get Firigin to teach it to them.
- If the boat is on the water and the song doesn't seem to work, that means Inigo is a long way from water that can be reached from the Midland Sea. Tough luck. Try again later. And please carry the boat back up the hill. He'll handle the tarp and illusion magic later.
- If asked, Firigin has no problem showing the PCs where the boat is kept, though he'll claim that all his secrets are used up and that's another reason he can't use the boat. He'd love to hear someone else's secret.

ICON RELATIONSHIP RESULTS

Feel free to use floating icon relationship results around Firigin if the PCs become interested in the interaction and start making things happen. Maybe Firigin isn't as retired from the invention business as he claims, or maybe he has a home-modified magic item kicking around that's associated with one of the icons. An icon relationship result of a 6, with some sweet-talking or intimidation, might get a PC an adventurer-tier item related to their icon somehow. A 5 has the same result, but, unbeknownst to the PC, the item will have a 50% failure rate. Whenever a battle begins, the tweaked-item will only have a 50% chance of functioning that battle, and the PC won't know that failure is possible until the item goes to sleep with an audible whine just as combat begins.

SILVER COVE

If the PCs follow Firigin's advice, they can find the boat. It's in mint condition. It smells like a fine magic item that is itching to be used. Adventurers know that smell.

It's a bit of a chore to haul the wooden boat to the water, but nothing too problematic unless you want to run another montage about little problems the PCs face carrying it for comedy relief.

A few lines into the *Ballad of the Stone Girl*, the boat judders to life with a comforting harmonic vibration, as if ready to take on passengers. The PCs fit comfortably into the boat. It seems like there would be room for another two or three people, but not more than that.

THE VOYAGE

When everyone is aboard, the boat begins moving of its own accord. No sail. No oars. Just steady propulsion out to sea and on into the mist. Paranoid PCs will be happy to know that it handles well. Potentially seasick PCs will not be happy to learn that it rolls a bit, but experienced sailors will tell them that the boat is actually magically stable, pitching far less than the waves would ordinarily require.

If the PCs haven't realized it already, they will soon: they aren't entirely certain where they are headed. And there still won't be any way of figuring that out!

But after a couple hours at sea, the boat is going to tell them! In the voice of a dwarven woman, the boat will announce: *"Destination confirmed: the Stranglesea."* That's all the boat will say. And an hour later, in a softer voice, it will repeat the same words again, and so on, every hour until the voyage is finished.

We'll cover other possible events on the journey in a moment. First, let's fill the PCs in on what some of them already know about the Stranglesea and find out if their resources or backgrounds can provide them with any other information.

THE STRANGLESEA?

What knowledgeable PCs are likely to know about it: The Stranglesea lies in the Midland Sea. A mat of tangled seaweed and captured flotsam so dense you can walk on it in places, it supposedly stretches for miles. Ships get trapped in it, sometimes permanently.

What everyone with a relevant background knows about it (no check required; break up between players if possible, and into bite-sized bits prompted by player questions):
- The currents drive sea plants from across the ocean, where they then attach themselves to one another, forming a great mass.
- The Stranglesea has existed for so long that new types of plants have arisen there. These intertwine, binding the seaweed mat tightly together.
- Bugs, worms, and crustaceans feed off the mass and each other; some types have only been found in the Stranglesea, making it a source of fascination to sages of the natural order.

- No one knows much about it because it's extremely difficult to find on purpose. Legends say that you find it on accident, or it finds you.
- It traps ships in a way that no ordinary skiff of seaweed would.
- Although you can walk on it, gaps appear in the weed mat, and bits of it connect only loosely to the main mass. One misjudged step, and you'll find yourself in the drink.
- Colonies of fish gather under the mat's shelter, a certain percentage of them predatory. These may bite you if you fall in.

13 Other Possibilities

These are other rumors about the Stranglesea that PCs may have heard or may hear if they find ways to talk with people/spirits as their boat plows through the waves. Other than entries 2, 4, 5, and 11, these rumors are probably untrue or irrelevant to the adventure, and are thrown in for additional flavor. That doesn't stop you from using them as springboards for improvisation if the group decides to expand its Stranglesea explorations, or if icon relationship rolls drive the narrative in unexpected directions.

1: A race of albino sahuagin, banished by their parent communities, dwells on the weed mat. Having lost the ability to breathe underwater, they fiercely defend their pathetic scraps of living territory.

2: Being trapped in the Stranglesea for too long drives a sailor mad.

3: The High Druid blames the Archmage and Emperor's wards for creating an unnatural half-alive zone in the middle of the sea.

4: Goblins, fleeing the servitude of evil icons, dwell in the hulls of ruined ships across the weed mat.

5: Killer whales patrol the waters around the weed mat. They've been known to knock over small boats to attack the inhabitants. They'll go after swimming gnomes and halflings, mistaking them for seals.

6: One can navigate at night around the Stranglesea by following the glowing outlines of luminescent sharks, which circle the weed mat in a predictable pattern.

7: The Stranglesea floats above the place where the sea elves used to live. No one, not even the Elf Queen, talks about the sea elves any more, as if they never existed.

8: Songs composed on the Stranglesea ache with melancholy or induce a crushing feeling of oppression. When the famous bard Urntur Urntursson sang a ballad he wrote there before the healing priestesses of the White Temple, they fell upon him, disemboweled him, and stuck his head on a pike.

9: The current Prince of Shadows ascended to the role after leaving his predecessor out in the weeds. He doesn't want anyone to find the body ....

10: The doubloon crab, about an inch across, filters tiny gold particles from the water, helping to form its shell. Prized as jewelry components, they are found only in the Stranglesea.

11: The experimental dwarven vessel *Sea Hammer* disappeared while on a mission to break up the weed mat once and for all. It's not entirely clear why the Dwarf King cared, but he did. Or the dwarves on the *Sea Hammer* thought he did.

12: The mermaids there might look like mermaids, but they're really plant creatures.

13: The Stranglesea is all that remains of the last Sea Sultan, a capricious, proud icon who exists in some ages and not in others. If the age turns and a new Sea Sultan arises, the seaweed will serve as the placenta of this terrible rebirth.

Reaching the Stranglesea

The wonders of the journey from the Silver Cove to the Stranglesea might include:

- a school of dolphins leaping from the sun-kissed ocean
- a treacherous plunge up and down black waves in the midst of a punishing storm
- the sight of a distant, primal battle between squid and sperm whale
- passing a glittering elven trade vessel, its sails shimmering like gossamer

Option A: Describe these, and/or other vignettes of your invention, long enough to convey a sense of transition and a several-day journey. Skip more complications and get to the heart of the adventure, arrival in the Stranglesea.

Option B: If your players greatly enjoyed the travel montage on the way to find Firigin, you could run another. Remind the players that the Midland Sea is fairly calm, as seas go, having been pacified by the first Emperor. But of course time is not on the Empire's side and the wards are fading, so who knows what surprises might have found their way into the Sea.

CHAPTER THREE:

THE STRANGLESEA

Now we move from prelude to the core of the adventure.

ARRIVING AT THE STRANGLESEA

The edges of the Stranglesea's weed mat are festooned with the wrecks of ancient vessels. This junkyard of spars and debris helps hide the PCs' arrival from the weed mat's inhabitants, even if they sail up in the middle of the day.

The Stranglesea is many miles across, splayed across the horizon like a gently rolling island. The boat seems to know where it's going and heads straight for a peninsula that sticks out from the rest of the mass, aiming dead center and slipping in between old wrecks and great burls of seaweed. Remember that the boat is not really under the PCs' control; it docks where it wants to dock, pulling itself up onto the mat and then juddering to a halt, more or less hidden on the side of an old wreck covered in seaweed.

Careful groups may want to hide the boat. Let them. Exceptionally careful groups may want to see if they can use the gnome wizards' spell that Firigin borrowed. Sounds like a DC 15 skill check involving magical talent, but make sure they yell a new secret aloud! With a DC 20 on the skill check, they might hear gnomish laughter quickly cut off afterward ....

YOUR TEMPORARY HOME:
THE WEED MAT

The weed mat varies in thickness from eight to thirty inches. Gaps in the mat, which become less common as you head toward the center of a weed island, allow you to look down into the calm waters below. The darting of small fishes and crabs, feeding on the weeds, lends flashes of movement to the otherwise stilled waters.

The mat gives off a loamy, seawater smell, with a faint undertone of decaying fish and plant matter. Thread-thin carnivorous plant tendrils reach out from the edges of the gaps to pierce the bodies of unlucky fish. Other fish join the plants in feeding from them.

When stepping on the weed mat, water audibly squishes up around the explorer's boots. The mat sinks noticeably, making travel across it an unsteady affair—compare it to walking across a waterbed. (Obviously that's a metaphor for players, not an in-character reference.)

Moving silently across the mat requires a hard (DC 20) Dex check. Though precarious, it offers a flat surface, without rises or bumps. The only obstacles to sight lines are the innumerable ancient ships trapped in the mat ... as well as a couple newer vessels and their inhabitants that will be encountered soon.

NOTHING TO SEE HERE

The old wrecks have been picked over, eaten through, and slimed. There's nothing of true value on them. For characters that insist on searching, here's a sample list of the kinds of things they'll find. You can use the list for any random search event on the Stranglesea if the PCs avoid messing about on the wrecks: *brass buttons too slimy to pick up properly; splinters that leave oozing red welts; weird pulsing coral that looks like it should be underwater; eyeball half hidden in the weed mat that is alive and seems to watch you wherever you move, though it's not clear what the eyeball belongs to, and it shuts and dies if messed with; super slimy green seaweed that's a different color of green than the rest of the weed mat; disgusting nest of some foul bird; broken bottle; untraceable bizarre odor that comes back whenever you stop looking for its source.*

SHARK PLUNGE

As soon as the entire party has stepped onto the mat for the first time, call for Dex checks. The PC with the lowest modified result (even if successful) falls through the mat and into the water below. Through gaps in the mat, the characters see the dark, slowly cruising shape of an enormous shark, then witness its abrupt acceleration toward the splashing character.

The first character to attempt to retrieve the fallen comrade makes a normal (DC 15) Dex check. *Success:* the character is rescued, with just a moment to spare, as the shark's toothy maw rises through the hole in the mat, then vanishes back into the depths. *Failure:* the shark takes a bite out of the character, who takes 2d6 damage.

This is an unconventional trap, in that the character who potentially suffers the harm is not the one with the chance to avoid it. It establishes unease about the Stranglesea environment. Having done this once, you're unlikely to find a good reason to repeat it. *Describing* sharks moving under the mat, on the other hand, may help to keep the group focused on forward movement.

SWIMMING UNDER THE WEEDS

At some point, for example in an attempt to circumvent the fencing around the dwarven perimeter (see page 24), the heroes might choose to break through the mat at one location, swim below the mat to a second spot, and then tear their way up through that. Predatory marine life adds a bracing element of danger to this otherwise clever move.

Each time characters go for a prolonged swim under the mat, they run the risk of a bite from a randomly determined sea animal.

BITER TABLE (D12)

1–4:   Orca
5–6:   Barracuda
7–12: Shark

Anything other than a barracuda lunges for one party member only. If the group took measures to make one of their number a more attractive target, the creature obliges and bites the designated bait. Otherwise, at your creative discretion, it targets a) the character whose player seemed most sanguine about the possibility of a bite; or b) a random PC. **+5 vs. PD**—2d6 damage.

Barracuda attack in a school, targeting all swimmers. **+5 vs. PD**—1d10 damage.

Does this scene feel like it requires more jeopardy? Once the character arrives at the chosen exit point, the mat proves particularly hard to penetrate. The weeds might be densely woven. Maybe a sizable chunk of ship deck occupies the desired spot. The character trying to break through must make a hard (DC 20) Strength check to break through the mat or take drowning damage. **+5 vs. PD**—2d6 damage for one swimmer, 1d10 apiece if more than one character is under the water waiting to break through. Even in the event of a failed check, the hero still breaks through the mat—just not before getting a lungful of brine.

TERRAIN FOR DRUIDS

Not surprisingly, the Stranglesea always counts as swamp/lake/river for druids with the Terrain Caster talent. In addition, when night falls on the Stranglesea, inform each druid with Terrain Caster that they feel a connection to cave/dungeon/underworld magic. The connection starts at sunset and ends each sunrise.

FIGHTING ON THE WEEDS

The Stranglesea gives you a twist on the classic grouped encounters formula. It combines the fresh air and natural imagery of the wilderness adventure with a room-like structure equivalent to a dungeon.

The tedious way to make players feel that their characters are fighting in a novel environment would be to force additional skill checks on them, with damage and other drawbacks as the cost of failure. That would slow down play and upset the encounter math.

Instead, weave the hazards of the weed mat into your fight narration.

When **a creature scores a natural 20 on an attack, or a PC rolls a natural 1 on its attack**, describe the PC target as suffering a mat-related additional mishap.

When **a creature gets a natural 1 on its attack or the PC attacking it scores a critical**, describe the creature suffering the same.

These mishaps do not cause any additional damage, or induce conditions. Treat them as flavor only.

Example mishaps, expressed from a PC's point of view (rephrase them into the third person for creatures):

- You plunge feet-first through the mat:
  - wrenching a muscle
- dropping an item needed later, outside of combat (either on the mat, for later retrieval, or in the water, if you describe the character recovering it as part of the same action)
  - and are stung by a jellyfish
  - and are bitten by a barracuda, small shark, or other predatory fish
- You land on the mat and are:
  - burned by caustic plant secretions
  - bitten or stung by insects, crabs
  - stabbed by a sharp piece of ship wreckage, like a shard of planking, a grappling hook
- You fall face-first through the mat:
  - and gulp down a lungful of seawater
  - (or modify some of the above mishaps)

Do the players seem disappointed that they're not further penalized after a mishap? Assign them a –2 penalty on all checks until the end of their next turns.

Do they seem disappointed that the creatures aren't further penalized? Play them a sonata on your tiny violin.

WANDERING WEEDBEAST ENCOUNTER

Throw these at the group whenever a mobile opponent seems appropriate. Maybe the group is wasting time endlessly discussing their next move instead of making it. Perhaps the session timing cries out for a sudden fight, even though the group is nowhere near a site-specific opponent.

WANDERING WEEDBEAST FIGHT CHART

Number of PCs	Weedbeast Shamblers	Weedbeast Trappers	Weedbeast Slammers	Weedbeast Stumblers
4 (Fight #1)	2	2	0	0
5 (Fight #1)	3	2	0	0
6 (Fight #1)	2	2	1	0
4 (Fight #2)	0	2	1	2
5 (Fight #2)	2	2	0	6
6 (Fight #2)	2	2	0	12

WEEDBEASTS

Every so often the cursed energy of the Stranglesea reaches a critical mass, giving temporary form to roving creatures that coalesce from the seaweed. Capable of hunger if not sentient motivation, these shambling weed-forms seek to absorb nutrients from any organic targets their heat-seeking senses detect. All of the mat's residents must deal with periodic eruptions of weedbeast activity, except for the fungi, which the weedbeasts sense as being part of the mat.

WEEDBEAST SHAMBLER

1ˢᵗ level troop [PLANT]
Initiative: +2

Smashing pseudopod +6 vs. AC—5 damage, +1d6 damage vs. stuck targets

Tougher from afar: The weedbeast shambler gains a +2 bonus to all defenses against ranged attacks.

AC	16	
PD	13	HP 27
MD	12	

WEEDBEAST TRAPPER

1ˢᵗ level spoiler [PLANT]
Initiative: +2

Slimy pseudopod +6 vs. AC—5 damage
  Natural even hit: Target is stuck (save ends).

Parting is such agonizing sorrow: Targets that successfully save to end the stuck condition caused by the *slimy pseudopod* attack take 5 damage.

Tougher from afar: The weedbeast trapper gains a +2 bonus to all defenses against ranged attacks.

AC	16	
PD	12	HP 27
MD	13	

WEEDBEAST SLAMMER

2ⁿᵈ level wrecker [PLANT]
Initiative: +2

Slamming pseudopod +8 vs. AC—9 damage

Opportunistic strike: The weedbeast slammer gains a +2 to all attacks against stuck targets.

Tougher from afar: The weedbeast slammer gains a +2 to all defenses against ranged attacks.

AC	17	
PD	15	HP 36
MD	12	

WEEDBEAST STUMBLER

0 level mook [PLANT]
Initiative: +1

Feeble pseudopod +5 vs. AC—3 damage; 5 damage vs. stuck targets

AC	16	
PD	14	HP 5 (mook)
MD	10	

Mook: Kill one weedbeast stumbler for every 5 damage you deal to the mob.

POLITICS IN THE WEEDS

Three factions inhabit the particular weed peninsula where our main action takes place:

- Sea goblins, who live in the stern of the wrecked ship *Forbearance*.
- A motley collection of wreck rats, sailors of the various major sentient races, formerly the crew of the *Forbearance*.
- Paranoid dwarves, survivors of the stranding of the experimental vessel *Sea Hammer*, now trapped in it.

All of them hate and fear the others. Each group has spent years preying on the others, thinning the ranks of all.

Goblins remember life nowhere else; as intergenerational weed-dwellers, they recount legends of the great forefathers who dared to sail the ocean, in search of freedom from the commands of callous icons. They regard the other groups as interlopers on their sacred territory.

Do you want to mess with your players' sympathies, as the author of this adventure is wont to do? Portray the goblins as unjustly put-upon victims of encroaching invaders, whose resort to savagery occurs in self-defense.

Do your players just want some uncomplicated monster-slaying? Play these goblins in their typical contemptible villain role.

The wreck rats arrived next. They've been in the weeds for nearly three years, having lost occupation rights to half their vessel as soon as it got caught here. Over the years, they've gone from desperate to crazy, not to mention slightly mutated.

The dwarves have been trapped for about nine months, long enough to retreat into their own truculent variety of insanity.

The one thing all groups agree on is that they'd be better off without the others.

The adventurers may be tempted to negotiate with the dwarves and wreck rats, who at first glance might appear like suitable allies. The value of diplomacy depends on how the PCs choose to approach them, which in turn affects where you place Inigo Sharpe.

None of the factions give the group any credit for attacking another group before talking to them. That advantage has already been granted; why risk or give away anything for it, when they can bank it for free?

The goblins agree to parley only if the PCs present themselves from a position of strength. Decide what this means depending on how the group plays it. The goblins might respond fearfully, and thus be willing to talk, if the group shows up on their doorstep fully rested. Alternately, the adventurers might make themselves appear formidable even when they've been whittled down, on a suitably described Cha check. The goblins just want their entire weed patch back, and try to convince the group to dispose of the dwarves and wreck rats. If they sense that the party will do their dirty work for them, they promise to trade Inigo Sharpe for that service, whether they have him or not (see below).

Unless you count shouted insults, the dwarves refuse to talk to the group if it does anything to interfere with their perimeter fence (see "Dwarven Perimeter") or potentially damage their ship. Their primary goal is to activate their ship's engines again and free themselves from the weeds. As a secondary goal, they want the goblins and wreck rats gone, because either of them might interfere with their first goal. They don't trust fancy talkers, nature lovers, or anyone who might be an agent of the Prince of Shadows.

The wreck rats want the heroes' boat, so they can escape the Stranglesea and return home. As they scheme toward that end, they'll also steer the adventurers toward their secondary goals. If the adventurers seem especially formidable, they'll steer them toward attacking the dwarves, whom they are too weak to take out themselves. If they don't see the heroes as being able to accomplish a task of that magnitude, they'll urge them to attack the less well-defended goblins.

FACTIONS AND ICONS

The group's openly expressed icon affiliations may affect their interactions with the three factions, who have opinions of their own regarding certain of the icons.

Like all right-thinking **dwarves**, the crew of the *Sea Hammer* loathes the Elf Queen and Prince of Shadows. One of these two sabotaged the ship, they're sure of it. It's the sort of job the Prince would get up to, but protecting these stupid weeds is the sort of cause she would support. Maybe they did it together!

The dwarves want to earn their way back into the Dwarf King's good books on their own. Although they'll swear up and down that they're absolutely loyal to him, they jealously seek to undermine anyone who actually is.

Goblins despise all icons as oppressors, especially the evil ones. Over all else, they want to avoid the notice of any icons, who they imagine are all scheming to re-enslave them. Mention of any icon relationship may spiral into a frenzied surprise attack.

Wreck rats claim to crave the rescue the merciful Priestess might grant them. However, if presented with the chance to flee, they'll resist with the crazy ferocity of cornered animals. Other than that, they blame whatever icons they once followed—primarily the Emperor, whose ships they served on—for abandoning them like this.

THE CURSE

The three factions agree on one thing: the Stranglesea is more than just a collection of weeds. Though individually inanimate and insensate, its choking plants and its chunks of jetsam form together into some ill-defined collective entity. The Stranglesea's dark soul ensnares the minds of its inhabitants just as its weedy tendrils seize onto pieces of floating wreckage. In their various ways, the wreck rats, dwarves, and goblins all speak of its curse. Those who stay here too long start to commit acts of irrational violence and self-destruction. You can tell when the curse settles on a person—the eyes glaze over, the jaw goes slack, the mind jettisons all conscious thought. Usually you wake up after a few

minutes, often in a terrible fix. Maybe you wind up on the edge of the mat, ready to jump off into an orca's jaws. Or you wander into sea elephant territory, unarmed.

Each group offers its own explanation for this.

The goblins say that their demigoddess of the sea, Glarkar, wants them to seize the entire weed mat—not just this bit, but all of it—for themselves. She punishes them because so far they have been too weak, too outnumbered, to execute her bidding. By increasing their numbers and driving off all others, they can lift the curse. Militant goblins believe they'll be the generation to undo the shame of their stupid forebears and accomplish this deed. Despairing ones bemoan Glarkar's unreasoning demands, which in their own way are just as bad as the icons their ancestors came here to escape.

Dwarves say that the Stranglesea embodies the putrefying corruption of nature gone awry. That's why they came here in the first place, to destroy its chaotic influence on the world. Naturally now that it has them trapped, it works to plant the seeds of doubt in their minds.

Wreck rats don't explain the curse. They just know that it exists. It's the force that warped their forms and impelled their companions to suicide.

THE CURSE GETS TO WORK

After the heroes' first encounter in the Stranglesea, the curse starts to work on them. Call for normal (DC 15) Wis checks. Those who fail realize that a part of them wants to stay here on the weeds. Forever. This doesn't affect their behavior, unless the players choose to embrace these weird thoughts and make decisions as if their characters are succumbing to them. Instead, describe it as a second set of alien thoughts suddenly intruding on normal consciousness.

After a second encounter, call for another round of Wis checks. Suggest that the player with the worst Wis result, even if it would normally be successful, roleplay a slight loss of mental control. If the cursed PC has relationship points with more than one icon, ask them which icon they feel distant from here on the mat. Temporarily remove one icon relationship point with that icon, or with the PC's only icon, if they have only one icon, and replace it with a temporary relationship point with the Stranglesea! Ignore any 5s or 6s that die rolls; instead, if it comes up as a 1, the PC is going to do something during the session that seems pretty insane, like drinking things they shouldn't, slapping a weird mutant sea star onto their face, or feeding one of their fingers to the crabs. You get the picture. On a 2, the PC talks about doing this type of thing but will only go through with it if the other PCs ignore them or can't talk them out of it.

In ascending order of Wis checks results, have one player per subsequent *session* follow suit. Cursing a character every battle is too harsh, but if the PCs dawdle too many sessions on the Stranglesea, they'll all be cursed at least a little.

SHARING RESPONSIBILITY

You don't have to take responsibility for all the icon relationship results. Particularly when the PCs are trapped on the weed mat with all the cursed Stranglesea crazies, feel free to make your players responsible for coming up with ways that the power or luck of their icons could work in their favor in order to implement one of their successful icon relationship results. Especially when things go wrong for the PCs, suggest that the power of an icon might be able to turn the situation around ....

PLACING SHARPE

Delay deciding where the heroes can find Sharpe until the last possible moment, to give the PCs reason to engage in as many of the Stranglesea combat encounters as you can manage.

If the group goes on a straight-up series of raids without talking to anyone, the choice is simple—he's found in the last encounter, whichever that winds up being.

If they talk to the intelligent mat inhabitants before attacking them and one of the characters has a background, unique thing, or other item or ability allowing them to see through deceptions, you might have to decide earlier, when an NPC makes a claim about his whereabouts that the heroes are able to test.

The goblins and wreck rats might say they have Sharpe, even though they don't, to get the heroes to attack their foes. Conversely, they might say they don't, when they do, if the adventurers have earned their distrust or anger.

If the dwarves have Sharpe, they won't let him go, because they hope they can use his engineering expertise to rebuild their ship. Since this is an imperative matter, they don't consider it dishonorable to issue a curt denial. Their self-righteous honor prevents them from pretending to have Sharpe.

Will lie if they:	Dwarves	Goblins	Wreck rats
Do have Sharpe	Yes	Possibly	Possibly
Don't have Sharpe	No	Possibly	Possibly

If this edge case forces you to decide, think about the current state of affairs and guess which answer will most enable you to make maximum use of the Stranglesea encounters.

Are your players the types who want their characters to wipe out all the creatures on the map? Don't bother to make any complicated calculations in placing Sharpe. They'll take on everything anyway. Even the elephant seals, who are just minding their own business.

Do your players feel a sense of accomplishment when they cleverly duck a combat? You might instead set up the adventure so that a choice they make and/or victory they score before leaving for the Stranglesea gives them correct information on Sharpe's location, allowing them to skip some of the fights.

BRINGING IN ICON RELATIONSHIPS WITH SHARPE JETSAM

When Sharpe washed up on the weed mats, one or more of his works-in-progress perhaps floated there along with them. These can be found on the mat, satisfying relationship rolls to icons not otherwise involved in the main storyline. Finding one or two of these items during the course of the adventure will be interesting and hint that the player characters are on the right track. Finding more than three would wear out the novelty.

If any of these items are found, they show up during:

- mop-up sequences, as the heroes scour an area in the wake of an encounter
- scouting sequences, as they explore an area as the prelude to an encounter

If you're paying off a roll bringing in a positive relationship, pick the appropriate entry from the positive relationship header. For rolls invoking negative relationships, pick an entry under that header. For conflicted relationships, ask the player to roll a die: even rolls get an item from the positive list; odd, from the negative. Or let the player decide whether she finds something that could hurt the icon (in which case use the negative list) or help (positive).

Though wondrous, these are less personal magic items than they are plot hooks to develop characters' icon relationships. Where otherwise unspecified, a positive item impresses any representatives of the icon who see you carrying it. It earns you even greater favor if you gift it to them. A negative item, if detected, offends the icon's representatives, causing them to lash out against you.

Some of these items reprise ideas from the list of possible plot hooks at the beginning. This is okay because you're ignoring relationship rolls to the patron and antagonist icons, who are already getting plenty of play as the drivers of your main storyline.

By default, the character finding the item has heard of it already from his brushes with the icon in question, and understands its significance, something to do with life back in the Empire, nothing to do with this squalid weed mat. Ask the player: *You've heard of this thing, though you didn't know it had anything to do with Sharpe. How did you learn of it?*

Alternately, you could leave the item's purpose and relevance a mystery for the moment. In a later session, once back on the mainland, the icon learns the players have it and through the usual layers of intermediaries either offers thanks or tries to gain it by force or guile. This keeps the backstory creation to a minimum, which for players who find it hard to dream up plot details on the spot might be a plus. On the other hand, it does delay the invocation of the icon roll.

POSITIVE RELATIONSHIPS

 A pendant featuring a translucent egg with a tiny automaton of snake eating its own tail. Allows its wearer to work through the night without suffering mental strain, increasing intellectual acuity to a peak in the hour before dawn.

 A partially constructed anti-demon blade, with whirring clockwork blades. The Crusader's people will want this. Even more, they want Sharpe to finish the design.

 A stone sextant. Anyone pointing this at a device of dwarven manufacture, or even a component thereof, knows what its original function was.

 A brass tiara with whirring discs. Grants restful sleep to the wearer, curing insomnia. If worn during the full moon, grants a lifelike dream of communion with the elven primal ancestors of the 1st Age.

 An elaborate miter with glowing gems. Feels weightless to any who genuinely love the Emperor. Quickly causes neck strain in those who regard him with indifference or ire.

 An animated figurine of a baby dragon hatching from its egg. Can be placed on all but the wispiest of clouds, which then supports its weight, and that of any flying creature that chooses to land on it.

 A steel band of variable circumference, with a snap to open and close. Wrap it around a sick tree for twenty-four hours, and it heals the tree.

 A key embossed with reversed symbols of various deities. Opens various locks altered by Sharpe to be otherwise inoperable. Among these are the coffers of the priory overseen by the Abbess Panutha (or another already established Priestess representative).

 A leather pendant featuring a mechanical eye. An incomplete prototype of a device that shields the wearer's thoughts from scrying. The Prince's people will want this. Even more, they want Sharpe to finish the design.

NEGATIVE RELATIONSHIPS

 A partly constructed set of goggles, with spikes inset to pierce the eyes of the wearer. This prototype device not only blinds the wearer but strips him of the power to cast spells. If completed, it would be a key weapon for any foe of the Archmage's. If the Imperial Wizardry School faculty get wind of it, they want it destroyed, along with anyone who could complete it. Maybe, some of them think, it would be safer to also eliminate anyone who knows about it.

 A mechanized brass mask with the features of a demon. Grants the wearer +2 to hit, and +2 AC against, any opponent who has ever killed a demon. Naturally the Crusader's forces take a murderously dim view of anyone wearing such a blasphemous contraption.

 A partially constructed anti-demon blade, with whirring clockwork blades. If completed, it would be a key weapon for the Diabolist's many foes. If she finds out about it, she'll want to destroy it, along with anyone who discovered it, worked on it, or so much as touched it.

 A stone torc covered in peculiar gold filaments. This prototype device, if completed, seals itself to the neck of an unwary wearer, creating a powerful compulsion to remain underground at all times, the deeper the better. If completed and produced in quantity, it could exile the top servitors of the Dwarf King to a strictly subterranean existence, limiting his power in the broader Empire. If his agents learn of it, they want it destroyed, along with anyone who had any part in making or distributing it.

 A prototype alembic for the distillation of green lotus philter, along with a partial recipe for its manufacture. Elves of a prior age saw their influence reduced when the court drank this concoction, which sapped its members of volition and pulled them finally into a death-like sleep. Absent from history for many ages, its return would strike horror into the Elf Queen's followers. They want it destroyed, along with anyone associated with it.

 Five gold rings, attached to one another by delicate silver chains. This prototype device turns its wearers against figures of authority, especially those they previously swore loyalty to. Sharpe made one but hasn't been able to replicate the process since. Its existence would terrify Imperial officials, striking as it does at the very heart of the relationship between an Emperor and his citizens.

A mirror framed in lacquered wood, into which the writhing forms of demons are carved. If you stare into this mirror while bleeding, you can see into the Abyss. Demons will shamble over to you and can engage you in conversation. The Wyrm's forces, who struggle all the time to stop more demons from entering the world, believe that nothing good can come of easy communication with their foul realm.

 An articulated brass locust. One of these prototype devices makes for an interesting curiosity. A hundred could be used to reduce an acre of forest into sawdust in the course of an afternoon. Sharpe originally made it for the Imperial agriculture ministry as a proposed means of quickly clearing land for farming. He gave up on it after they caught him diverting supplies to his immortality project. The High Druid's followers think they destroyed all of them, and will react with fury against anyone making the slightest move to resurrect this buried idea.

 A brass tube marked with various sigils representing life energy. This prototype wand, if completed, would become a powerful weapon against the undead. At present it merely emits an aura that makes the ambulant dead instinctively want to destroy anyone carrying it.

 An iron pyramid covered in peculiar dials. One of these alone doesn't do much, but a bunch of them in sequence creates a line of force that injures anyone crossing it. Built as a trap to protect frontiers from raiders, it would blunt the Orc Lord's dreams of conquest if deployed in large numbers. A hero encouraging Sharpe to return to this project attracts the violent ire of the Orc Lord's horde.

 A small ivory figurine of a four-legged fish, which waggles its tongue when warmed by the heat of one's hand. Sharpe claims that it diverts divine good fortune, taking the blessings of the deities from the faithful and giving them to the fish's owner. Or maybe it doesn't; he gave up the project because it was too hard to prove that it was working. However, the ecclesiastics consider the mere idea of it blasphemous, whether it works or not. Anyone owning one spits in the face of all that is holy, and must be brought to heel.

 A brooch, in silver studded with agates, in the shape of a human ear. Sharpe designed this item to punish deceivers. When perfected, it will work on anyone who touches it, even briefly. For months afterward, the subject will be unable to lie without succumbing to an obvious fit of sweating and twitching. Criminals and con artists will kill to stop its manufacture.

 A lattice of wires on the end of a three-foot metal stake. If perfected, this would warn of the approach of flying creatures. Especially useful at night, it would make raids by hostile dragons more difficult. When agents of the Blue and Black learn of it, they set out to destroy it, and anyone near it.

ENCOUNTER DIFFICULTY

The notes below show you how to calibrate the battles of the Stranglesea to suit the needs of the moment.

When it becomes apparent that an imminent scrap will likely be the last Stranglesea fight, make that an unfair combat, using the guidelines given in each encounter.

We do not present an unfair version of the Basking Zone / elephant seal fight. If it looks like that will wind up being the last battle, make the penultimate fight unfair—assuming you can see this coming in advance. Even a climactic showdown with fungus seems cooler than making elephant seals your boss monsters.

Due to the fortification effects, the Dwarf Perimeter encounter may already be a touch unfair. Drawing opponents in from the Unfair rows makes it doubly so.

ENCOUNTER FORMAT

Stranglesea encounters feature the following elements:

Environment: A description of the terrain, furnishings, and any other physical specifics the heroes will spot on first glance. Paraphrase or read aloud, in accordance with your usual habits.

Soft approach: What the inhabitants of the area, if any, are doing if they have no idea the heroes have arrived to maraud their way across this stretch of mat. In most cases a single fight will alert all the other inhabitants to the group's presence, allowing only one soft approach.

Hard approach: What inhabitants are doing if already aware of the group's presence.

Approach: The inhabitants either take no notice of the group's presence or take no measures to prepare for it. Substitutes for both the soft and hard approach entries.

Roster: This chart lists creature rosters for standard and unfair fights against 4, 5, or 6 PCs.

Battle notes: Miscellaneous details on how the fight might go down.

Creature stats then appear under their own header.

Sharpe: Where Inigo Sharpe is, if you've placed him in this area. This may indicate that he won't be found here, but in an adjacent area controlled by the same faction.

Plot threads: Notes on noncombat interactions that might occur here.

Treasure: If you're abstracting the treasure, as is *13ᵗʰ Age*'s usual wont, ignore this. Instead, at the adventure's conclusion, the patron disburses loot pegged to the number of encounters the group undertook.

On the other hand, if the players seem invested in scoring loot on the scene, this entry shows what they find. At the adventure's end, the patron disburses treasure only in accordance with any encounters before or after the Stranglesea.

GOBLIN CAMP

Environment: Fish bones litter a thick stretch of seaweed mat. Depending on the PCs' approach, the goblins may not be in plain view, so when the PCs do manage a clear view, emphasize that these are some creepy-looking goblins! Some have webbed hands, others have head-crests like frilly coral, and others have fish eyes and scales.

Soft approach: Rotting, sea-scourged benches sit along the sea shore formed by the mat's western edge, along with a couple of likewise battered tables. Three campfires glow from points throughout the mat. Shivering goblins huddle around them. It's hard to tell from a distance, but the fires appear to be built on steel sheets, shielding them from the damp. The goblins chatter in low, sulky voices. They haven't spotted you yet, but not far below their postures of bored relaxation, you can tell they're alert for signs of danger. They seem most prepared for trouble from the south, without much attention paid to threats coming from the water.

Hard approach: Rotting, sea-scourged benches and a handful of tables have been arrayed as shields against enemy encroachment. Three large steel plates lie at intervals across the area, each one blackened with the soot and dusty white coals of recent fires. Behind the benches you see the helmets and weapons of crouching figures bracing for a scrap. Though stamped with an unfamiliar accent, their guttural mutterings give them away as goblins.

ROSTER: GOBLIN CAMP FIGHT CHART

Number of PCs	Goblin Grunts	Goblin Fish-Witchers	Goblin Slashers	Goblin Curse Victims
4 (Fair)	2	1	0	5
5 (Fair)	2	1	0	10
6 (Fair)	2	2	0	15
4 (Unfair)	2	2	0	15
5 (Unfair)	2	2	1	15
6 (Unfair)	3	2	1	15

Battle notes: On a hard approach, the goblins crouch behind the benches and tables, firing ranged weapons, until overrun. Attacks to hit them are at −2 until they're flushed from cover.

In your narration of combat events, characters or creatures might:
- knock over, throw, or smash a bench or table
- slam into a campfire, or the metal remains of an extinguished fire

GOBLIN GRUNT

1ˢᵗ level troop [HUMANOID]
Initiative: +3

Club +6 vs. AC—6 damage if the goblins and their allies outnumber their enemies; 4 damage if they don't.

R: Shortbow +6 vs. AC (one nearby enemy, or a far away enemy at −2 attack)—4 damage

Shifty bugger: Goblins gain a +5 bonus to disengage checks.

AC	16	
PD	13	**HP 22**
MD	12	

GOBLIN FISH-WITCHER

Flying fish abound here, sometimes leaping from the water to accidentally hit a victim with stunning force. This self-taught shaman has learned to make them do it on purpose.

1ˢᵗ level archer [HUMANOID]
Initiative: +5

Elephant seal tusk club +6 vs. AC—4 damage

R: Summon flying fish +6 vs. PD—5 damage
Natural 16+: The goblin fish-witcher deals 3 + the escalation die damage to the next nearby enemy to roll a natural odd attack (from another leaping flying fish!).

Shifty bugger: Goblins gain a +5 bonus to disengage checks.

AC	16	
PD	11	**HP 25**
MD	15	

GOBLIN SLASHER

2nd level troop [HUMANOID]
Initiative: +3

Club +7 vs. AC—8 damage if the goblins and their allies outnumber their enemies; 5 damage if they don't.

R: Shortbow +7 vs. AC (one nearby enemy, or a far away enemy at −2 attack)—5 damage

Shifty bugger: Goblins gain a +5 bonus to disengage checks.

Twist of the knife: On a successful disengage check, the goblin slasher deals 3 damage to every opponent it was engaged with.

AC	17	
PD	14	HP 29
MD	13	

GOBLIN CURSE VICTIM

Not a victim of a goblin curse, but a goblin accursed by the Stranglesea effect.

0 level mook [HUMANOID]
Initiative: +2

Club +4 vs. AC—3 damage

R: Shortbow +5 vs. AC (one nearby enemy, or a far away enemy at −2 attack)—3 damage

Shifty bugger: Goblins gain a +5 bonus to disengage checks.

AC	16	
PD	14	HP 5 (mook)
MD	11	

Mook: Kill one goblin curse victim for every 5 damage you deal to the mob.

Sharpe: If the goblins have Sharpe, he's in the ship.

Plot threads: For goblin negotiating positions, see "Politics in the Weeds," previous. With this group, a fish-witcher named Grazk does the talking.

Other goblin names, if needed: Gruk, Glorn, Gleg, Glak, Gron, Glothag.

Treasure: 7 gp per character in the form of scrap precious metal.

GOBLINS & FIRE!

A couple of our playtesters commented that in their games, goblins didn't use fire. *13ᵗʰ Age* campaigns interpret the details of cultures and monsters differently, so if your goblins are way different than the goblins on the weed mat, chalk it up to another effect of Stranglesea mutation.

GOBLIN SHIP

Environment: A door sawed into the side of the vessel offers entry to the goblins' salvaged shelter. The dried skins of luminescent fish cover the interior of this shattered sailing vessel, granting it faint illumination. Sheets crudely sewn from rancid rags hang about the hull, dividing it into sections. The reek of rotten fish oil assails your nostrils. A pile of broken crates plugs the breach in the ship's hull, which points to the north. A network of rafters and catwalks made from scavenged wood has been nailed semi-skillfully into place, filling the top third of the hull. These sit about twelve feet off the ground. The total height of the hull is eighteen feet.

Soft approach: (Possible only if the heroes negotiated their way in.) Goblins cautiously approach you, jabbering to one another in their assonant tongue, beady eyes glittering with a mix of hope and terror. A lithe goblin wearing a shark's lower jaw, the key feature of her headdress, steps forward to bang the haft of her trident on the hull floor, as if it is a holy implement. "What boon do you seek of us?" she croaks.

Hard approach: Goblins who didn't want to join the fight outside hide in the rafters of the ship, hoping that the heroes will wander in and allow them to leap on them with surprise, surrounding them. A goblin blade acts as the ambusher, nominating another as an ally if available, a three-pronger if not. The jellyfish thrower(s) stay in the rafters, throwing jellyfish, until engaged or pulled down.

ROSTER: GOBLIN SHIP FIGHT CHART

Number of PCs	Goblin Three-Prongers	Goblin Blades	Goblin Jellyfish Throwers	Goblin Curse Victims
4 (Fair)	2	1	1	0
5 (Fair)	2	2	1	0
6 (Fair)	2	2	2	0
4 (Unfair)	2	2	1	0
5 (Unfair)	2	2	2	0
6 (Unfair)	2	2	2	3

Battle notes: Jellyfish throwers attempt to get distance on the fight to lob in their missiles. They might:
- climb into the rafters
- or retreat to the north end of the ship, where they then knock down the wall of crates, leap over the other side, and fire into the ship from the edge of the fungus patch

Other interactions with the environment you might narrate into the fight:
- A combatant gets tangled in the rag curtains.
- A sheet of luminescent fish skin is torn off the wall, covering someone's face.
- The crate stack collapses, in- or outward.
- A crate spills open, revealing a carefully polished store of dwarf and wreck rat bones.

GOBLIN THREE-PRONGER

1st level troop [HUMANOID]
Initiative: +3

Trident +6 vs. AC—5 damage, and the goblin three-pronger pops free after its first successful attack and after all subsequent attacks on a natural 16+

Thrust: The goblin three-pronger gains +2 with this attack when targeting an opponent for the first time in this battle.

R: Shortbow +5 vs. AC (one nearby enemy, or a far away enemy at –2 attack)—4 damage

Shifty bugger: Goblins gain a +5 bonus to disengage checks.

AC	16	
PD	13	**HP 26**
MD	12	

GOBLIN JELLYFISH THROWERS

After taking dozens of stings from the toxic jellyfish that float around the Stranglesea, these furtive goblins build up an immunity. They keep the creatures in buckets, to hurl at invaders.

1st level troop [HUMANOID]
Initiative: +3

Trident +5 vs. AC—4 damage, or 6 damage against opponents currently taking ongoing damage

R: Jellyfish throw +6 vs. AC—4 damage, plus 4 ongoing damage

They want to know what the jellyfish does: If no *jellyfish throw* attack by any jellyfish thrower has succeeded, and the escalation die exceeds 1, the jellyfish thrower gains a +6 bonus to *jellyfish throw* attack.

Shifty bugger: Goblins gain a +5 bonus to disengage checks.

AC	16	
PD	13	**HP 24**
MD	12	

GOBLIN BLADE

1st level spoiler [HUMANOID]
Initiative: +3

Bone dagger +5 vs. AC—4 damage, and target takes 6 damage on any failed disengage check (save ends)

Shifty bugger: Goblins gain a +5 bonus to disengage checks.

AC	15	
PD	14	**HP 28**
MD	13	

GOBLIN CURSE VICTIM

Not a victim of a goblin curse, but a goblin accursed by the Stranglesea effect.

0 level mook [HUMANOID]
Initiative: +2

Club +4 vs. AC—3 damage

R: Shortbow +5 vs. AC (one nearby enemy, or a far away enemy at –2 attack)—3 damage

Shifty bugger: Goblins gain a +5 bonus to disengage checks.

AC	16	
PD	14	**HP 5 (mook)**
MD	11	

Mook: Kill one goblin curse victim for every 5 damage you deal to the mob.

Sharpe: If Sharpe is here, he's stored in one of the crates. The goblins periodically remove him from his imprisonment to demand prophecies and weather forecasts. For more, see "The Dread State of Inigo Sharpe."

Plot threads: The goblins want to be alone on this patch of floating weeds, which they regard as their invaded homeland. If the heroes dispose of both the wreck rats and dwarves, the sea goblins might hold a celebration in their honor. This could turn into a fight if the adventurers offend their hosts by refusing to eat their wretched grub or drink their burning home brew. Or simply if they start to look more appealing as victims than as saviors ....

Even more goblin names: Glala, Glot, Gradak, Grent, Gekka, Glerinck

Treasure: 40 gp per character in the form of jewelry stripped from the corpses of dead wreck rats.

BASKING ZONE / TRASH HEAP

Environment: A mostly deserted stretch of weed flat, with a moldering heap of refuse at its northern end. It's not entirely clear which group of weed dwellers has been using this as a place to dump trash. If asked, the different groups blame each other, and there's garbage that might have come from each of the groups.

Soft approach: Elephant seals bask in the sun south of the trash heap.

Hard approach: Elephant seals arouse themselves from basking to bellow angry warnings.

ROSTER:

As many elephant seals as party members.

Battle notes: The seals try to herd their enemies into the trash heap. Someone falling into the heap might emerge covered with muck. Or with an alarming-looking parasitic worm or enormous insect stuck to them.

To nasty this up, a seal might forgo its damage on a 16+, instead bulling its target into the water, exposing her to a predatory shark strike; see "Swimming under the Weeds," page 14.

A fight against ordinary animals may at first seem oddly mundane for this adventure. In playtest, though, the group's reluctance to tackle them provided much entertaining interaction. Was it moral to kill animals who are just being animals, defending their turf? Would elephant seals kick their asses? The reluctance made the eventual fight, which they waded into after not finding the full-sized human Sharpe they were looking for among the dwarves, goblins, wreck rats, or fungi, a memorable adventure highlight.

Eʟᴇᴘʜᴀɴᴛ Sᴇᴀʟ

Though ordinary animals, these four to five ton beasts become wildly aggressive if you intrude on their territory. This is their territory.

1ˢᵗ level wrecker [ʙᴇᴀsᴛ]
Initiative: +3

Body slam +9—5 damage
Natural 16+: While remaining engaged with the target of its attack, the elephant seal also bull rushes another nearby opponent for 3 points of damage.

Nastier Specials

Mutant: This elephant seal is not so normal after all! As a reaction to being staggered, it unfurls a long mutated elephantine nose, spraying blood and noxious goo.
C: Elephant seal pus +9 vs. PD (the nearby enemy with the most hit points)—5 ongoing poison damage and confused (save ends both)
Limited use: 1/battle, as a free action after being staggered.

AC	14	
PD	11	**HP 27**
MD	8	

Sharpe: If he's here, he's buried deep in the trash heap. The goblins probably had him for a while, until he spooked them, prompting them to ditch his metallic head here. See "The Dread State of Inigo Sharpe."

Plot threads: It could be that the reason all three groups sometimes use the same trash heap is that the low-ranking members of each group who are assigned to take out the trash have worked out a half-functional system for trading things with each other in the trash. None of them really confess they're doing it, but taking out the trash isn't such a bad chore anymore, and there might be other interesting things half-hidden in the muck, possibly even including a piece of Sharpe's jetsam (page 18).

Treasure: 20 gp per character, in the form of a battered antique chalice stuck in the weed mat near the garbage pile.

Dᴡᴀʀᴠᴇɴ Pᴇʀɪᴍᴇᴛᴇʀ

Environment: A fence studded with razor sharp spikes forms a territorial boundary around an otherwise empty stretch of weed mat. From the center of the territory rises the exterior of a vast rusted ship. A blunt, hard-edged box of metal, the vessel looks like it should have been utterly unseaworthy. Ducts snake crazily across its flat prow and riveted sides. The mountainous sigil of the Dwarf King repeats as an embossed emblem between the riveted joins. A stylized emblem of his face gazes formidably out from the prow, as if willing the sea to obey the commands of the earth. Along its top edge runs a crenellated iron wall. (For the ship's interior, see next encounter entry.)

Soft approach: The area bounded by the fence is empty. You spot a watchman atop the ship, between crenellations, but he hasn't seen you yet.

Hard approach: As soon as anyone interferes with the wall or enters the perimeter, crossbow bolts rain down from behind the crenellated wall.

Rᴏsᴛᴇʀ: Dᴡᴀʀᴠᴇɴ Pᴇʀɪᴍᴇᴛᴇʀ Fɪɢʜᴛ Cʜᴀʀᴛ

Number of PCs	Dwarf Crossbows	Dwarf Sailors	Dwarf Officers
4 (Fair)	2	2	0
5 (Fair)	2	2	1
6 (Fair)	3	2	2
4 (Unfair)	2	2	1
5 (Unfair)	3	2	1
6 (Unfair)	3	2	1

Battle notes: Scaling the fence requires a normal Dex check (DC 15) that can be attempted once a round; on a failure, the character can use another move action to climb it anyway and accept 2d6 damage, or wait till next round to try again, when they might succeed in maneuvering around all the spikes. (In other words, characters going over the fence in a noncombat situation can just wait until they get it right and won't take any damage.)

It takes a round of exposure to missile fire to cross the perimeter and reach the ship.

Firing on the dwarves when they are behind their wall incurs the standard −2 attack penalty.

The ductwork on the vessel's surface allows heroes to clamber up the sides. This costs a standard action (not the usual move action) and requires a hard (DC 20) Strength check. Failure indicates slow progress; the character doesn't fall off the side, but must try again in a subsequent round. Success means that characters reach the top and can close to melee with the defenders as of the beginning of their next action. Accordingly, even if PCs succeed, they are still on the side of the ship for at least one round.

The defending dwarves can, as a standard action, activate a device that vents scalding steam off the side of the ship. Only PCs currently on the side of the ship can be targeted by this. The dwarf makes his **best attack roll vs. PD**; on a hit, the target takes 5 damage. On a natural 16+, a character having just made a successful climb check is considered to have failed and must try again next round.

Once the heroes make it up the side of the ship, the melee portion of the battle actually takes place atop its flat steel roof, not the perimeter area itself.

Under ordinary circumstances the dwarves stick to their defensive strategy and can't be lured off the top of the ship to fight in the perimeter or outside the fence. They'd rather fire on the adventurers every time they come poking around than expose themselves. Perhaps the players will dream up a crazy scheme that seems like it ought to smoke them out.

Dwarf Crossbow

1st level archer [HUMANOID]
Initiative: +4

Cutlass +5 vs. AC—4 damage

R: Crossbow +5 vs. AC (one nearby or far away enemy) —5 damage

AC	16	
PD	12	**HP 26**
MD	13	

Dwarf Sailor

1st level troop [HUMANOID]
Initiative: +3

Cutlass +6 vs. AC—5 damage

R: Crossbow +5 vs. AC (one nearby or far away enemy) —4 damage

AC	16	
PD	12	**HP 26**
MD	13	

Dwarf Officer

1st level leader [HUMANOID]
Initiative: +3

Cutlass +6 vs. AC—5 damage

Revered: When the dwarf officer takes 4 or more damage from an opponent's attack, all dwarves gain a +1 bonus to damage until the end of the next turn.

AC	17	
PD	15	**HP 26**
MD	11	

Sharpe isn't here, or on top of the ship, but might be inside it.

Plot threads: The dwarves made their fence back when their ship's engines, which powered the forge, still worked. They refashioned it from interior bulkheads, largely gutting their vessel. It can't be raised from a distance; nor is there a gate to walk through. Dwarves only leave the perimeter for rare sallies to the garbage heap. Conveniently enough, they dumped their garbage right before the heroes arrived and can't be accosted in a stakeout. If asked, they explain that one of their number, Egli, has become quite proficient in scaling the fence without getting impaled. He performs all the garbage runs, and has the elephant seal tusk scars to prove it.

So even if the dwarves invite them in, the adventurers still have to climb over the spiked fence.

Really, the dwarves would prefer to conduct any negotiations by shouting from atop their ship. The officer, called Meriden, does the talking—or, rather, yelling. Should they convince her they're worth talking to, she invites them in. Then they go inside the ship and have to negotiate all over again with the captain (see next encounter).

The dwarves want a way to restart their vessel, and otherwise to be left alone. A proposal to get rid of the goblins and wreck rats gets their attention, since that would lead to their being left alone in the future.

Other dwarf names, if needed: Boroks, Auberim, Thaudorim, Farul, Cirok

Treasure: 26 gp per character in the form of silver jewels in the dwarves' dreadlocks and beards.

DWARF SHIP

Environment: The ship interior has been mostly gutted, exposing the metallic skeleton of a once majestic, if thoroughly improbable, vessel. Riveted joists dangle from the ceiling. Pallets line the floor in one corner. Hissing gouts of steam, lit by fitful torchlight, obscure vision. Piles of parts and metal shavings lie in corners, as if subjected to constant but vain attempts to keep them in an orderly array. At the center of the ship, like a wounded beast rendered in metal, thumps a clearly damaged engine that now produces nothing but hot vapor clouds.

Soft approach: After passing muster with the officer, Meriden, the closest door opens, admitting the characters to the presence of the captain, Sangol. Weather beaten and extravagantly pierced and tattooed, he subjects the group to the full gruffness of his fatalistic attitude. For more on negotiating with the dwarves, see "Politics in the Weeds," previous.

Hard approach: If the heroes have taken out all the dwarves outside the ship, they then face the problem of getting inside it. A hard (DC 20) Int skill check opens one of the complicated mechanical doors, one on the east side of the ship and the other on the west. Or, if they're on top of the ship, they can pry up one of the two ventilation grates, which requires a normal (DC 15) Strength skill check. This requires a normal (DC 15) climb check (Dex), assuming they have the rope to do it with. And why wouldn't they? Failure incurs 5 damage, representing a twisted ankle or the like.

ROSTER: DWARF SHIP FIGHT CHART

Number of PCs	Dwarf Crossbows	Dwarf Skullcrushers	Dwarf Brawlers	Dwarf Captain
4 (Fair)	1	2	1	0
5 (Fair)	1	2	2	0
6 (Fair)	0	2	2	1
4 (Unfair)	1	2	2	0
5 (Unfair)	1	2	2	1
6 (Unfair)	1	2	3	1

In encounters that don't list the captain as a combatant, the part of Sangol is played by a skull basher.

Battle notes: Crossbowmen take up sniping positions behind the engine. Depending on positioning, this cover may levy a –2 penalty on attacks against them.

A missed conventional missile attack by one of the heroes might hit the engine, sending additional steam shooting through the ship interior. The dwarves cry out in rage: their only means of escape has been further damaged! Their fury costs them –1 on attacks but grants +2 damage on all hits.

Describe clanging weapons, thudding boots against metal, echoing shouts, choking humidity, and sweat beading on the brows of wearying battlers.

DWARF SKULL BASHER

1st level wrecker [HUMANOID]
Initiative: +2

Hammer +6 vs. AC—5 damage

Starts strong: The dwarf skull basher gains a +1d6 bonus to damage until the escalation die exceeds 2.

AC	17	
PD	15	**HP 28**
MD	11	

DWARF BRAWLER

1st level wrecker [HUMANOID]
Initiative: +2

Head butt +6 vs. AC—4 damage

Natural odd hit+: The dwarf brawler deals an additional 1d6 damage but is dazed until the end of its next turn.

AC	16	
PD	14	**HP 32**
MD	12	

DWARF CROSSBOW

1st level archer [HUMANOID]
Initiative: +4

Cutlass +5 vs. AC—4 damage

R: Crossbow +5 vs. AC (one nearby or far away enemy)
—5 damage

AC	16	
PD	12	**HP 26**
MD	13	

DWARF CAPTAIN

2nd level leader [HUMANOID]
Initiative: +3

Cutlass +6 vs. AC—5 damage

Revered: When the dwarf captain takes 4 or more damage from an opponent's attack, all dwarves gain bonuses of +2 to attack and +6 to damage until the end of their next turn.

AC	18	
PD	16	**HP 35**
MD	12	

Sharpe: If the dwarves have Sharpe, they keep him as a captive repair consultant. He has assisted them with their repairs, though not enough to restore the engine. If asked, Sharpe correctly insists that this is impossible, given the lack of parts. Never mind what he says—the dwarves see him as their best bet for restarting the ship and won't give him up willingly.

If they don't have Sharpe, they did at one time and want him back. They tell the party where they think he is—this might be the goblins or the wreck rats, depending on where you want to nudge things.

Once the heroes have Sharpe, a force of dwarves tries to ambush them to retrieve him. They'll even leave the safety of their ship and perimeter to do so.

Plot threads: Fixing the *Sea Hammer* should be next to impossible—but even as first level adventurers, the PCs' combination of unique things could make them specialists in the impossible. This requires the players to:

• come up with a Crazy Plan That Just Might Work
• make at least 3 ridiculously hard (DC 25) skill checks

Should they do this, describe the frenzied efforts of Sangol and company to test the engine, and then the ship's triumphant detachment from the weed mass. This could destabilize the entire seaweed island, sending it, and everyone left on it, plunging into the sea. Give the players a chance to guess at this possibility and safely place themselves either on their own vessel or inside the *Sea Hammer*.

Do the heroes like the wreck rats who have now been left behind? They might rush to save them from the sinking weed island. Or, in a campaign of cruel ironies, the heroes might watch in horror as their good deed dooms a bunch of hapless bystanders. This may provoke conflicted banter within the group, as friends of the Priestess quail and Crusader-positive types grunt with implacable fatalism.

Do the heroes hate the wreck rats? Seeing them vanish beneath the waves plays as an additional sweetener to their victory.

Need even more dwarf names? Vranav, Tharmun, Kerith, Colum, Maena

Treasure: 32 gp per player, in the form of tools made from precious metals.

FUNGUS PATCH

Environment: Except for some weird lumpy shapes sticking out of the weeds, this looks like an abandoned section of weed flat. But with every other stretch of the seaweed island fiercely occupied, maybe there's something weird about that. And maybe those lumps bear a closer look.

Approach: On that closer look, the heroes see a bubbling mass of not-quite-plant, not-quite-animal matter growing out of the weeds, in roughly globular pustules anywhere from six inches to four feet in diameter.

A normal (DC 15) Int check allows a party member to identify these as dangerous fungal masses from a safe distance. Otherwise, the group's most-likely nature expert remembers the lore about them when they coalesce to attack.

ROSTER: FUNGUS PATCH FIGHT CHART

Number of PCs	Fungal Flingers	Fungal Assemblages	Fungal Growths
4 (Fair)	2	1	3
5 (Fair)	2	1	6
6 (Fair)	2	2	6
4 (Unfair)	2	2	6
5 (Unfair)	2	3	6
6 (Unfair)	2	3	9

Battle notes: This fight revolves around attempts to disengage from the fungal masses when they seem ready to pop. With that tactical distinction, you won't need to work too hard to keep the fight interesting with narration. A few goopy details will go a long way. Be sure to make slurpy explosion noises when the creatures blow up.

FUNGAL MASSES

These predatory spore masses resolve into temporarily humanoid shape to kill large prey, like yourself. Their victims become the soil for new spores to grow. When a sudden blow disrupts the internal integrity of the spore mass, it turns into a choking cloud, then dissipates.

FUNGAL ASSEMBLAGE

1st level wrecker [PLANT]
Initiative: –1

Pseudopod slam +6 vs. AC—6 damage

Puffball anatomy: When reduced to 0 hit points, the assemblage deals 2d6 damage to any opponents engaged with it. (Tell the players about this up front, so they can respond tactically.)

Structurally unsound: The fungal assemblage is killed instantly by any critical hit.

AC	17	
PD	14	**HP 28**
MD	11	

FUNGAL FLINGER

1st level archer [PLANT]
Initiative: –1

Pseudopod slam +5 vs. AC—4 damage

R: Toxic spore puff +7 vs. MD (one random nearby enemy)—4 damage, and if target is cursed by the Stranglesea, target is confused (easy save ends)

Puffball anatomy: When reduced to 0 hit points, the flinger deals 2d6 damage to any opponents engaged with it. (Tell the players about this up front, so they can respond tactically.)

Structurally unsound: The fungal flinger is killed instantly by any critical hit.

AC	17	
PD	14	**HP 28**
MD	11	

FUNGAL GROWTH

1st level mook [PLANT]
Initiative: –1

Pseudopod swipe +6 vs. AC—4 damage

Puffball anatomy: When reduced to 0 hit points, the growth deals 1d3 damage to any opponents engaged with it. (Tell the players about this up front, so they can respond tactically.)

AC	16	
PD	14	**HP 4 (mook)**
MD	11	

Mook: Kill one fungal growth mook for every 4 damage you deal to the mob.

Sharpe: If Sharpe is here, he was recovered by a wreck rat or goblin who took an ill-considered shortcut through this area and was killed. Sharpe's disembodied brass head sits inside the last of the fungal masses to explode. It hurtles through the air at the PC who seems the most fitting subject for a moment of indignity. The force might knock the character off his feet, though without doing any real harm.

Plot threads: There's nothing and nobody to interact with here—unless you decide that the group needs a new entrée to one of the three groups. In this case, they find a barely breathing mat inhabitant the fungal masses were feeding on when they arrived. Her name is:

- Glara (goblin)
- Nachiri (dwarf)
- Arna (wreck rat)

She wandered into the fungal patch under the malign influence of the place and its curse. She explains that its curse sometimes prompts longtime castaways to self-destructive acts. Still weakened, she needs to be carried if she's going to get out of here before the masses reform. She promises to put in a good word for the group if they escort her home.

Treasure: 25 gp per character in the form of coins scattered through the fungal mass.

WRECK RAT CAMP

Environment: A stretch of weed mat strewn with tables, benches, and chairs. Four barrels line the outermost weed mat, not far from a doused campfire.

Soft approach: Disconsolate-looking people of various common races slump in chairs and on benches. The worn remains of sailor's garb hang off their emaciated frames. Something seems wrong with them, their postures contorted, their features marred. Some drink from battered tin flagons, while others just stare off into space.

Hard approach: Wretched members of various common races stand alert, weapons ready, against your incursion. The worn remains of sailor's garb hang off their emaciated frames. Something seems wrong with them, their postures contorted, their features marred. They mutter and growl—some in fear, others with sadistic anticipation.

ROSTER: WRECK RAT CAMP FIGHT CHART

Number of PCs	Wreck Rat Harpoon Fighters	Wreck Rat Swashbucklers	Wreck Rat Harpoon Throwers	Wreck Rat Starfish Faces
4 (Fair)	1	1	2	0
5 (Fair)	2	1	2	0
6 (Fair)	2	2	2	0
4 (Unfair)	2	1	2	0
5 (Unfair)	2	2	2	0
6 (Unfair)	2	2	2	1

Battle notes: Combatants might fall into or over the benches, tables, and chairs. The barrels on the edge of the mat contain a terrible-tasting and worse-smelling seaweed mash in various stages of fermentation. The wreck rats react in comic horror or righteous fury if this precious resource gets spilled. In a lighthearted campaign, they can shout insults in pirate accents.

When the fight starts to go against the wreck rats, the heroes see the ones inside the ship girding themselves for battle. Evidently they're going to let their comrades go down, then join the battle fresh and ready, giving the PCs no chance to rest between scraps.

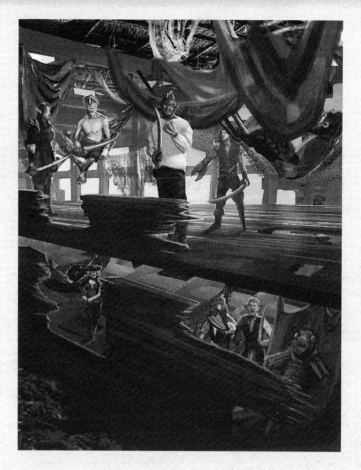

WRECK RAT HARPOON FIGHTER

1st level troop [HUMANOID]
Initiative: +3

Out-of-balance harpoon +6 vs. AC—5 damage
Natural 16+: The target is stuck and can become unstuck by taking an additional 4 damage.

R: Thrown dagger +5 vs. AC—4 damage

AC	17	
PD	15	**HP 27**
MD	11	

WRECK RAT HARPOON THROWER

1st level troop [HUMANOID]
Initiative: +3

Dagger +5 vs. AC—4 damage

R: Harpoon +6 vs. AC—5 damage
Natural 16+: The target is stuck and can become unstuck by taking an additional 4 damage.

Haul 'er in!: As a standard action, the harpoon thrower can pull a target it has struck past a nearby ally; the ally gets an opportunity attack against the target.

AC	17	
PD	15	**HP 26**
MD	11	

WRECK RAT SWASHBUCKLER

1st level blocker [HUMANOID]
Initiative: +3

Cutlass +6 vs. AC—5 damage, and a nearby ally may pop free

R: Thrown dagger +5 vs. AC—4 damage

AC	17	
PD	15	**HP 27**
MD	11	

WRECK RAT HARPOON MASTER

2nd level troop [HUMANOID]
Initiative: +3

Harpoon +7 vs. AC—7 damage
Natural 16+: The target is stuck and can become unstuck by taking an additional 5 damage.

R: Thrown Dagger +6 vs. AC—5 damage

AC	18	
PD	16	**HP 36**
MD	12	

WRECK RAT STARFISH FACE

Has a psychic starfish parasite fused permanently to his skull. Other than that, he's doing fine.

1st level caster [HUMANOID]
Initiative: +3

Dagger +5 vs. AC—4 damage

R: Domination +6 vs. MD (one random nearby enemy)— Target is confused until the end of its next turn.

AC	17	
PD	11	**HP 23**
MD	15	

Sharpe: If the wreck rats have Sharpe, he's inside the ship, not here.

Plot threads: The players may deem the wreck rats their best shot at an initial diplomatic sally. Their main goal is escape. While trying and mostly failing to be subtle about it, their self-appointed spokesman here, the thoroughly drunk but wily swashbuckler Clendennon, tries to learn how they got here. When it becomes apparent that there's no room for the wreck rats on the PCs' ship, the wreck rats start scheming to find and steal it. The easiest way to do this is to convince the PCs to attack first the dwarves and then the goblins. If the PCs reveal the general location of their boat, the wreck rats promise to protect it with all their honor as sailors. Lay it on thick enough that the players realize they're apt to steal the vessel if left alone with it.

Despite Clendennon's pretensions, the rest of them treat Moreau, from the ship, as their acting captain. To make a true alliance with the wreck rats, they'll have to deal with her.

Other wreck rat names, if you need them: Pirko (halfling or gnome), Wehoi (elf), Hask (half-orc)

Treasure: 26 gp per character in the form of assorted scrimshaws.

STEALING THE MAGIC BOAT

The boat can only return to Silver Cove, and only restarts if the song of the Stone Girl is sung. So the wreck rats can't steal it.

Surely the heroes won't be so rash as to tell the wreck rats how to start their magic boat!

But it might be possible to damage the boat. Smart player characters won't have tried that, so how could they know?

You can create suspense around this prospect, but, remember that if the heroes do lose the boat, you'll have to invent a credible alternate way off the weed island.

Maybe that dwarf ship can be revived after all ....

WRECK RAT SHIP

Environment: Hammocks and dried weed curtains convert the hull into small components offering a modicum of privacy. A large wooden wash tub in the middle of the room holds a pile of dry clothing, implying that it isn't used as often as desperate close-quarters living might call for. Along the top of the hollowed-out hull hang cords, also made from dried seaweed. Presumably these would be used as clotheslines if anyone here saw fit to wash their decaying outfits.

Alongside more robust-looking wreck rats loll another half dozen clearly too far gone to lift a cutlass. Obviously ailing, they lie in their hammocks, watching events through a haze of pain. All show symptoms of transformation into sea creatures: hands fusing into fins, gills sprouting on necks, or scales sprouting from skin.

Soft approach: The only possible soft approach sees the group escorted in by Clendennon. If the parley later goes sour, the group has allowed itself to be outnumbered by two encounters' worth of foes.

Hard approach: If the group attacked the wreck rats outside, this second shift lies in wait for them, after they've been softened up by their fallen comrades. If the heroes retire after beating on the first group of wreck rats, these ones charge, to catch them before they heal up.

ROSTER: WRECK RAT SHIP FIGHT CHART

Number of PCs	Wreck Rat Swashbucklers	Wreck Rat Hook-Hands	Wreck Rat Starfish Faces
4 (Fair)	2	1	1
5 (Fair)	2	2	1
6 (Fair)	2	2	2
4 (Unfair)	2	2	2
5 (Unfair)	3	2	2
6 (Unfair)	3	2	2

Battle notes: Some of the pathetic noncombat wreck rats might be hurt or killed by collateral damage in the fight.

They might act as a chorus, shouting abuse at the heroes.

If you decide to turn a battle unfair by introducing reinforcements midway through, they burst out of the tub, having hidden in the pile of clothes until a tempting moment to strike.

WRECK RAT STARFISH FACE

Has a psychic starfish parasite fused permanently to her skull. Other than that, she's doing fine.

1st level caster [HUMANOID]
Initiative: +3

Dagger +5 vs. AC—4 damage

R: Domination +6 vs. MD (one random nearby enemy)—
Target is confused until the end of its next turn.

AC	17	
PD	11	HP 23
MD	15	

WRECK RAT HOOK-HAND

1st level troop [HUMANOID]

Initiative: +3

Hook +6 vs. AC—5 damage, and the target suffers a −4 penalty on checks to disengage from the wreck rat hook-hand until the end of the battle

R: Thrown dagger +5 vs. AC—4 damage

AC	17	
PD	15	**HP 27**
MD	11	

Sharpe: If the wreck rats have Sharpe, they keep him under the pile of clothes in their tub. They believe he acts as a magic talisman slowing the progress of the dread magic transforming them into creatures of the deep. He denies this, but he would, wouldn't he?

Plot threads: The acting captain, Moreau, is one of the starfish faces. Mournful and gloomy, she thinks herself already doomed and might be ready to go out in a blaze of bloody glory. On the other hand, she cares enough about her people to want to get the relatively healthy ones to safety, if that is possible. She'd steal the heroes' boat in a heartbeat in order to arrange that. If she likes them, she'll feel remorse about it, but it won't stop her from trying.

Other wreck rat names: Zabba (gnome), Mockley (halfling), Elberil (elf), Starmast (human)

Treasure: 27 gp per character in the form of scattered coins and personal jewelry.

CHAPTER FOUR:

THE DREAD STATE OF INIGO SHARPE

Inigo Sharpe is now not a man but a consciousness stored in a brass replica of his former, living head. Articulated eyes roll around in metal sockets; a clacking mouth moves up and down when he speaks. His voice emanates from the brass head, which lacks a tongue, larynx, or vocal cords, by magical means. Its ghostly tones echo eerily in its hearers' heads.

TIMING THE HEAD REVEAL

Placing the revelation of Sharpe's condition as far into the Stranglesea section as you can allows you to employ an entertaining misdirect. If the heroes enter one of the three possible locations for it on peaceful terms, they can inspect the joint, conclude that Sharpe isn't there, and continue clearing out the weed mat's other areas. Forced to go back and search again, they find out he's a head and have to complete the last encounter. The alpha playtest group followed this pattern with the dwarves, and the revelation played as a classic twist, landing with the inevitability of all great narrative surprises.

Sharpe wants to return to civilization, specifically to a safe place the antagonist icon cannot reach. As far as he's concerned, the patron icon's protection seems as good a bet as any. Once able to work in peace, he intends to reconstruct an automaton body to screw his hollow neck onto, returning to a semblance of independence, if not biological life.

A self-proclaimed genius, he considers his exile here a profound humiliation. When asked how he got here and what happened to him since he was last heard of in the Empire, he tries to change the subject. In response to specific questions, Sharpe provides the information given in the bullet points below. Even as he tells the tale, he reveals himself as somewhat of an ambiguous character. If dragging him back to work for the group's client seems unfair, he also appears to deserve it.

To reduce the chance that you'll be caught flatfooted and have to make something up on the fly, this section provides more details than you need to introduce. Most groups will only fish for exposition relevant to the plot hook you used to draw them in. And also where any extra treasure might be. Don't prod them to drag the whole thing out of Sharpe. If much of this remains unrevealed after their curiosity runs out, that's not just fine but good.

- Over the years, he worked for various clients, mostly tied to the heroic and ambiguous icons. (He doesn't use the game terms, but rather names them if asked.) Although he did build and invent devices they wanted, or at least made an honest stab toward them, he always secretly squirreled away lore and supplies to complete his real task—achieving immortality for himself.
- His relations with clients follow a familiar pattern: high hopes, followed by disenchantment and a messy break, after they failed to accord him the respect he deserved.
- Often the villainous icons would try to capture him, to force him to work on projects of destruction.
- Yes, yes, he left poor Firigin somewhat in the lurch when he left. But one cannot shackle oneself to plodders of limited ambition. No discoveries would ever get made that way!
- He set up his own secret, independent lab, then got to work on his immortality device—a metal golem's body that his soul and awareness could migrate to upon his death.
- When he ran out of funds for the immortality project, he announced that he was working on the device that triggered the antagonist icon's wrath (seen in chapter one, "Sharpe and the Enemy"). He offered it up to the highest bidder.
- Before any buyers could step forward, the forces of the antagonist icon came and slew him.
- With his project incomplete, his soul migrated into the automaton's discorporate brass head. The rest of him had yet to be built.
- A treacherous lab assistant, the accursed Chalko, missed the massacre and figured out what had happened. He seized Sharpe's head and arranged to sell it to yet another icon. (Pick an icon from the currently outstanding icon relationship rolls.)
- Chalko's ocean journey to a rendezvous with that icon's agent ended in a terrible storm that sunk his ship.
- Thanks to its revolutionary buoyant design, Sharpe's head bounced along the waves until it became entangled in the Stranglesea. Sometime later the wreck rats, goblins, or dwarves found him and claimed him as treasure.

Whoever had Sharpe here in the Stranglesea mistreated him. They all had him at one time or another, whatever they may have told the party.

Do any wreck rat, dwarf, or goblin encounters remain? Before Sharpe leaves, he angles for a taste of revenge. If it looks like the group plans to exit the island without killing every intelligent creature on it, he comes up with a story in a bid to persuade them. Should they resist, Sharpe establishes a psychic link with his invention, the ship, preventing it from moving. The team can overcome this with improvised magic or by bringing appropriate backgrounds or unique things into play. This requires a normal (DC 15) check, probably of Int or Wis. Or they can just clang Sharpe's head against the side of the boat, breaking his connection with it.

If so, they can sail into the sunset to the tune of his insults and imprecations.

Are the PCs still first level? Not anymore they aren't. Finding Sharpe and getting off the island merits advancement to second level. Nothing provides a visceral sense of accomplishment like leveling up.

Did your final battle read to the players as a suitably climactic conclusion? If so, jump to "The Delivery." Consider having the enemies listed in "Ambush" show up in a later session, mistakenly believing that they still have the head. This completes the setup given in the prelude without adding an extra fight you don't need right now. Look for a distinguishing spin to put on the fight, replacing the bit where combatants fight for possession of Sharpe's head (see below).

Has the group been working for an ambiguous icon? Consider the pros and cons of ending with "The Turnaround."

Does Sharpe's talk of a second icon interested in his head prompt the players to reconsider their delivery options? Jump to "Switching Horses."

Did your final battle fizzle, leaving players craving a bigger ending? Go to "Ambush."

AMBUSH

Summary: A mixed group of baddies led by a female bugbear schemer named Tano Flensing Claw has been waiting for the PCs. Evil archers are on watch and will let fly when the PCs land in Silver Cove; the rest of the villains join the fight when the PCs get to roll initiative.

Setup: Firigin's magic boat heads back to Silver Cove. As currently configured, it always and only takes you back to where it started.

If the players seem concerned or curious about this, Sharpe complains that Firigin fabricated this replica with an unimaginative fidelity to the original template. He kept in the return-trip feature, even though it was a stupid request of the client who commissioned the first version. He could reset it, but only by taking it apart over a period of several weeks. With someone to follow his instructions and act as a pair of hands for him. Naturally this is not possible in the short term.

If the players accept the return trip as a given, Sharpe feels no particular urge to narrate the boat's backstory at them.

The battle: Agents of the antagonist wait for them in ambush at the boat's predetermined location. They found Firigin and beat the location out of him. They have him waiting to be dragged out from behind a tree on the beach, bloodied and shackled. Now that his information has proven correct, they will feel free to execute him—after defeating the heroes and relieving them of Sharpe's head.

The enemies don't know when or even if the PCs will return with Sharpe, but they know this is where the boat should bring them. The archers are on guard; the other baddies are near enough to get involved when the PCs roll initiative. Note that the archers will wait until the boat docks to start firing; they don't know that the boat can't necessarily be turned around and sailed away—they want the PCs on the shore. Unless the PCs have been deliberately vigilant, the archers' attack is probably officially an ambush (*13th Age*, page 164). If you don't know whether the archers can pull off an ambush against your paranoid or hyper-vigilant PCs, make it a DC 20 skill check to spot the ambushers.

GRABBING SHARPE

This fight distinguishes itself by revolving around the struggle for possession of Sharpe's brass head.

If the heroes enter the fight without grabbing Sharpe, one of the enemy troops tries to use both its move actions to run to the boat and take him. If successful, the enemy attempts to flee the melee entirely while the other opponents block the heroes from pursuing him. A combat-grade fantasy rugby match may then ensue.

Anyone striking a combatant carrying the brass head knocks the head from the combatant's grasp on a natural 16+. This does not preclude any effects that roll would normally trigger.

The bugbear schemer, Tano, knocks Sharpe's head out of its target's grasp on a natural 14+.

Once the head falls, it rolls through the scrum. Any combatant nearby to the character who dropped the head can pick it up by expending a move action. The combatant with the head can pass it to any other nearby combatant by expending a move action.

If the bugbear schemer gets the ~~ball~~, er, head, she makes a run for it while leaving her comrades behind as expendable blockers. They know better than to run after her, though they might surrender eventually if they think she got away safely.

OTHER FIGHT FEATURES

- Stray missile fire may strike and sink the boat.
- Ranged attackers can take cover in the willow branches, especially during the initial ambush shot. Attempts to hit them suffer the standard −2 disadvantage penalty.
- The melee might extend into the cove's shallow waters.
- If the PCs find a way to take to the water, Tano has a small boat of her own stowed nearby, but she's going to need someone to row until she can get the sail rigged.
- If Firigin is left alone once melee starts, he can chew through his gag with his fancy artificial teeth and start shouting warnings during the battle. It may just get him killed, or it may lead to mid-battle repartee between Firigin and Sharpe's head.

BATTLE ROSTER

As this encounter appears only to supply a big finish, it is built as an unfair fight only, and it assumes that the PCs have leveled up to second level.

To use it in a later session as a renewed plot thread after this adventure concludes, omit the bugbear.

As you adjust the enemy roster below, note that the bugbear schemer is the major threat, and always appears in the fight as the leader. You'll note that the other creatures are referred to by roles. You'll find two or three possibilities for each role below; choose the monsters you want appearing as agents of the enemy icon. Obviously the Lich King favors undead and the Orc Lord favors orcs, but anyone evil could employ humans or goblins or perhaps even an orc or skeleton.

AMBUSH FIGHTING CHART

Number of PCs	Archers	Troops	Casters	Bugbear Schemer
4	2	3	1	1
5	2	3	2	1
6	3	4	2	1

TANO FLENSING CLAW, BUGBEAR SCHEMER

Bugbears with the brains to run the show have a cruel streak that's sometimes darkly humorous. Some of the stories adventurers swap in taverns focus on hilarious insults that they took from bugbears they've fought.

3ʳᵈ level leader [HUMANOID]
Initiative: +7

Big-ass warclub +9 vs. AC—8 damage
Natural even hit or miss: Each of the bugbear schemer's nearby humanoid allies gains a +2 bonus to melee attacks until the start of the schemer's next turn.
Natural odd miss: 4 damage.

R: Ridiculously heavy crossbow +7 vs. AC (one nearby or far away enemy)—14 damage
Natural even hit: The target takes 1d6 extra damage.
Limited use: 1/battle.

[Special trigger] C: Rebuke to fools +9 vs. MD (one nearby enemy)—2d6 psychic damage
Limited use: 1/round as an interrupt action, when a nearby enemy rolls a natural 1–5 with an attack against it.

Combat reload: During the bugbear schemer's turn, if it doesn't engage an enemy or move, it regains a use of *ridiculously heavy crossbow* if it's expended as it reloads the crossbow.

Fighting withdrawal: When the bugbear schemer successfully disengages, one of the enemies engaged with it takes 1d6 damage.

AC	19	
PD	14	HP 42
MD	17	

ARCHERS

Choose archers that make sense for your evil icon, or mix and match.

HUMAN ARCHER

1ˢᵗ level archer [HUMANOID]
Initiative: +7

Short sword +4 vs. AC—3 damage

R: Bow +6 vs. AC—5 damage

Volley fire: If 2 or more human archers with the same initiative fire at the same target, each attack that misses deals 2 damage to a random nearby enemy.

AC	17	
PD	11	HP 27
MD	15	

SKELETON ARCHER

1ˢᵗ level archer [UNDEAD]
Initiative: +7
Vulnerability: holy

Jabby bones +5 vs. AC—4 damage

R: Shortbow +7 vs. AC—6 damage

Resist weapons 16+: When a weapon attack targets this creature, the attacker must roll a natural 16+ on the attack roll or it only deals half damage.

AC	16	
PD	14	HP 26
MD	11	

BEDRAGGLED ORCISH ARCHER

Some orcs think that bows stink of elvishness, and treat bow-wielding comrades accordingly.

1st level archer [HUMANOID]
Initiative: +4

Scimitar +5 vs. AC—4 damage

R: Short bow +5 vs. AC—5 damage
Natural 1–5: Reroll the attack against a random nearby creature. If the rerolled attack is also a natural 1–5, the orcish archer takes 3 damage from sheer agonized frustration, but it doesn't get to make another attack.

Final frenzy: When the escalation die is 3+, the orcish archer gains a +3 bonus to melee attacks and melee damage.

AC	17	
PD	14	**HP 22**
MD	10	

TROOPS

Choose a troop that make sense for your evil icon. If you feel like you want to make the battle tougher, adding another troop is a safe bet.

HUMAN THUG

1st level troop [HUMANOID]
Initiative: +3

Heavy mace +5 vs. AC—4 damage

Natural even hit or miss: The thug deals +6 damage with its next attack this battle. (GM, be sure to let the PCs know this is coming; it's not a secret.)

AC	17	
PD	14	**HP 27**
MD	12	

KOBOLD WARRIOR

1st level troop [HUMANOID]
Initiative: +4

Spear +8 vs. AC—4 damage
Natural even hit or miss: The kobold warrior can pop free from the target.

Evasive: Kobolds take no damage from missed attacks.

Not brave: Kobold warriors with single digit hit points will run away the first chance they get.

AC	18	
PD	15	**HP 22**
MD	12	

ORC WARRIOR

1st level troop [HUMANOID]
Initiative: +3

Jagged sword +6 vs. AC—6 damage
Dangerous: The crit range of attacks by orcs expands by 3 unless they are staggered.

AC	16	
PD	14	**HP 30**
MD	10	

CASTERS

If the hedge wizard was notable in the early fight, maybe you want to bring him or her back again. Otherwise, the shadowy ambiguous wizard person is your ticket.

HUMAN HEDGE WIZARD

1st level caster [HUMANOID]
Initiative: +3

Dagger +4 vs. AC—3 damage

R: Fire jet +4 vs. PD (one nearby or far away enemy)—4 damage
Natural even hit: Each enemy nearby the target takes 1 spillover damage.

AC	16	
PD	12	**HP 26**
MD	15	

SHADOWY AMBIGUOUS WIZARD PERSON

Cloaked, always in shadows, blandly unremarkable until spells begin melting people's faces off.

1st level caster [HUMANOID]
Initiative: +5

Wavy dagger +3 vs. AC—4 damage

R: Dark bolt +6 vs. PD (one nearby or far away enemy)—7 negative energy damage
Miss: The *dark bolt* deals 3 damage to a random nearby ally of the shadowy ambiguous wizard person!

AC	15	
PD	13	**HP 30**
MD	14	

SHIP ABANDONERS

It's barely possible that the PCs will want to leave Firigin's boat early, avoiding the return to the boat's home beach. That's probably more likely if one or more of the players has heard what happens at the end of the adventure. Ditching the boat early is a fine and paranoid maneuver. Given that Sharpe is now away from the interfering magic of the Stranglesea, it's possible that the would-be ambushers will track him down somehow. Even if the ambush is entirely canceled rather than postponed to a later session, the PCs should hear about the consequences of their evasion. Firigin has probably been slain by angry villains. On the other hand, he might have joined with the villains and figured out how to make powerful changes to the boat, which in this case should be played up as a powerful magical artifact the PCs let out of their hands.

ENDINGS
THE TURNAROUND

You could skip the ambush and still end with a lethal battle. Agents of an ambiguous icon might turn triumph into defeat, prompting the heroes to plot ongoing revenge that might reverberate through the rest of the campaign. In this option, the ambiguous icon-tied retainer betrays them after they deliver Sharpe's head to the contact. Once it is safely in hand, the retainer orders henchmen like the ones above (but not the same characters) to kill the players, so they won't blab word of this to rivals.

Personally I wouldn't do this—it ends an escapist escapade on a bummer note, and it's a gaming cliché to boot.

But maybe your players take perverse pleasure from being torqued around by your cruel GMing, or doing so sets up something you need for your longer-term story.

SWITCHING HORSES

GMs aren't the only ones to indulge a propensity for backstabbing. Depending on what they asked Sharpe, the heroes might show their skeevy sides, realizing that another icon also wants the head. Maybe they can get a better deal from this other prospective. Perhaps more of the players are aligned with that icon than they are with the patron. It could be that they've angered that other icon and could really use a peace offering.

This player-directed sequence could lead directly from a safe landing, or occur after the ambush.

THE DELIVERY

In the straight-up ending, the players bring the head of Inigo Sharpe to their designated contact, who thanks them, compliments their cleverness and valor, and rewards them with treasure commensurate with the number of fights they've undergone. (Modify this reward downward if they've been successfully looting, old-school style, along the way.)

The contact makes it clear that they appreciate the work the team has done for them, and will be in touch with future missions to test their mettle and fill their purses.

FORESHADOWINGS

Running *The Strangling Sea* sets in motion a number of potential plot lines. You might seek player cues to work out which of them they find interesting, or hit them with the ideas that get your own imagination going.

- The client gets Sharpe to work on whatever project is described in the plot hook you chose. Sharpe needs a rare metal or alchemical ingredient to complete his work. Naturally, this can only be found somewhere dangerous, or can be gained in trade for the completion of some other mission. The client assigns the heroes to get the item or execute the needed favor.
- Sharpe sends the group a message smuggled from the redoubt of whichever client they wound up delivering him to. He's discovered an imminent threat to the Empire, one he can only stop if sprung from the grip of his short-sighted possessor.
- Firigin comes to them with breathless news—the being inside Sharpe's automaton head isn't Sharpe, but a demonic replica. He tried to reach and warn the icon who owns the head but was brushed off. Can the heroes investigate and prove Firigin right? Or is it all a scheme to slake Firigin's thirst for vengeance, now surprisingly rekindled?
- If the PCs want the magic boat to do magic for them, they're going to have to perform errands for Sharpe as payment for activating the vessel. Firigin would love to help, if he's still alive, but Sharpe reprogrammed the boat to his commands, not Firigin's.
- If the group recovered one or more pieces of Sharpe jetsam, its plot implications kick into gear.
- Sharpe assembles himself a new body and, as usual, scarpers from his client with work uncompleted. The group must once again retrieve him—but this time, he's a moving target.

✝HE WORLD WON'✝ SAVE I✝SELF.

Prophecies fail. Demons invade, living dungeons rip towards the surface, and the Empire's protectors falter. The great icons who shape the world arm for war.

So what's it going to be, heroes? Risk everything to forge your own epic history? Or grab the best loot and escape into the shadows?

13th Age is a d20-rolling fantasy game of battle, treasure, group storytelling, and heroic adventure.

For Players:
- Your character's "one unique thing" ensures there's no one else like you.
- Alliances and enmities with icons such as the Archmage, Lich King, and Prince of Shadows give your character a place in the world's story, even at first level.
- Streamlined and flexible combat rules create fast-moving, free flowing battles.
- Character backgrounds let you invent the stories that shape your skills.

As a GM:
- Design monsters and adventures quickly.
- Surprise yourself and your players with plot hooks from characters' backgrounds and unique features.
- Improve any d20-rolling game with mechanics such as the escalation die and incremental advance.

13✝H AGE:
FORGE HEROES.
SHAPE ✝HE WORLD.
BE LEGENDARY.

Get this from your friendly local game store!

$44.95

www.pelgranepress.com

Pelgrane Press

FIRE OPAL